# The Stolen Newborn Baby in the Maternal & Child Health Clinic
# &
# Mother's Love To Find Dead Or Alive

## The Challenges of Martial Law, Bribery & Corruption
## for
## A Nation

**True Story**

**Dr. Badal W. Kariye (Hunbul)**

# Acknowledgments

This is a work of true story whose germs are developed and based on in the soil of my mother's memory, although the background of the events narrated here comes from other brains such as my mother, young sister and I who wrote it down whenever we chatted and shared about family issues.

However; I ought to make it very clear that any resemblances to actual persons, living or dead are purely coincidental.

I really thank to my mother who made it possible for us to know the truth about this true story, and how the newborn boy was stolen after giving him birth at Banadir Hospital in Mogadishu City, the Democratic Republic of Somalia. Every mother has to read and benefit from this true story so that they can help others who've either lost or their child had been stolen.

Positively, you'll learn a lot from this true story if you're still living under civil rule or military regime, and you can find solutions for survival and struggling daily until you're completely free from harms way.

Let's enjoy reading it!

II

# Author's Note

I'm Dr. Badal W. Kariye who is the legendary Somali American author of 43 previously published books, which have been interpreted into more languages and won numerous awards. I've accomplished my literary works at very young age, and I'm currently writing for a life.

I'm also a Martial Arts expert who enjoys to practice after I feel very tied for my writing schedules.

I speaks many languages, and I'm truly social philanthropist who volunteers whenever he has time to offer and serve the communities.

I am a motivational speaker, a life coach and community organizer whose talks focus on topics of life empowerment, security, spirituality, youth, social issues & public diplomacy. Well, I have more 24 years of experience in public service and engaging multicultural audiences focusing on civic and community activism as well as security and diplomacy.

I lectured to audiences across Africa, North America, Europe, Australia, Asia and Latin America.

And this book is my 44th Novel so, you can enjoy and read this true story.

III

# CONTENTS

# Chapter 1

Once upon time a mother gave birth to baby boy after long life threatening delivery complication at Banadir Hospital on December 15, 1969 in Mogadishu, Somalia. Unfortunately, after delivering her baby boy then she became unconscious.

After that one of the duty nurses took the baby boy to clean and place him at a cradle nearby his mother however; she has never returned to a room where the baby boy's mother was sleeping as unconscious person.

Willy-nily, the female nurse on duty decided to steal the baby boy while she did it intentionally. She wrote a note declaring that the baby boy passed away, and he was placed at the clinic mortuary for funeral arrangement.

She wanted to exchange my mother's baby boy with someone dead baby, and she brought the dead baby to nearby mother's bed with a red cradle and a big note hanging from it.

My mother woke up and asked for her baby boy!

"The duty nurse said," "My dead," "Your new child is dead."

My mother cried so much, and she said to the duty nurse that her new baby boy is alive. "The mother added," "Her son looks like his father," "She saw him before even she became unconscious." So, the duty nurse must bring her rightful baby boy.

I really saw my son! Are you a nurse? Or are you a smuggling thief?

The duty nurse started to get her stuff so she could leave the Banadir Hospital soon before my mother and her relatives calls the Somali Local Police State for criminal investigations. She ran away from the Banadir Hospital by taking Somali Yellow and Red Taxi to her friend's home where she kept the stolen baby boy.

Surely, Somali plainclothes man suspected her how she came out from the Banadir Hospital? Then he followed her up until she reached her friend's home which was localed at Wardigley District in Mogadishu, Somalia.

The plainclothes man wrote a note to his diary in case any case arises from the Banadir Hospital which took place during that night, and he kept it at his desk for 5 days to listen any bad news from the Banadir Hospital.

By the way, the duty nurse decided to leave Somalia before further investigations are carried out by the Somali Local Police Station which is locally knowns as the Casa-Balbalare Police State State then she bought a Somali Airline Ticket to abroad.

Undoubtedly, the Somali plainclothes officer heard that there was a rumor which a duty nurse at the Banadir Hospital stole a baby boy from unconscious mother whose husband was a high ranking Somali government officer.

Then the Somali plainclothes officer informed his superiors that he has already written note about this incident which occurred at Banadir Hospial on December 15, 1969 where he even personally following up a suspecting infirmed nurse in hurry.

I think that It is very true that the Somali plainclothes officer was either trying to seduce her or he wanted to know why she was in hurry? Anyway; the possibles are unlimited if and where state was governed martially.

Silently, the duty nurse seek how to contact and ask for some questions to the Somali plainclothes officer whom she thought that he knew some important information to incriminate her for further investigations.

“She could not find him,” “Because it was very hard to know or tell the exact name of many Somali plainclothes officers who used to work or patrol around the Banadir Hospital where many Somali military facilities including officer's housing located.”

To her understanding how dangerously she went to commit this criminal act? Then she went to visit one of Somalia's most feared palmist where she could get some information to help her escape nicely without further investigations.

After some nurses released that 3rd baby boy is now missing within 3 weeks from the Maternity and Child Health Clinic at the Banadir Hospital then they began asking for serious question about who steals babies?

And who is missing from the staff on duty?

Surprisingly, one of the duty staff nursed said clearly that she was the duty nurse in-charge has take a crying child out of his mother's room then she brought back a silence baby boy from the Clinic Mortuary to replace him, and that was what she thought!

“The nurse added,” “Well,” “Maybe, she never gave birth to a child.” If she did gave birth to a child then she would have know the painful delivery which most of the mothers go through during their first born.

“As one of the duty nurse staff,” “It is the best time to her our duty nurse in-charge before it is too late to handle this issue internally.”

“I mean it.”

Well, the Banadir staff gathered to ask for questions and get answers how easily are babies born at the Banadir Maternity and Child Clinic are stolen or missing? Some doctors shocked to listen one of the nurses exposing bad deals at the Banadir Hospital.

“She clearly confirmed that some of the nurses are not following the rules, and are paid enough to steal babies for selling them in the black market where many things happen where you like it or not.

“She stood up,” “She said to the Banadir Hosptial staf that she would prefer to leave her job because it is not secure to work in.”

“She smiled nicely,” She walked out.”

Many of Banadir staff including patients came to discuss  such criminal issues and how they safeguard children in the near future? They planned to host one of the biggest ceremonies ever held at the Banadir Hospital.

Surely, many of the Banadir staff and government officials attended the ceremony for reviewing incidents and carrying out further investigations to know how long? And how many children are missing?

What danger would they encounter? Maybe, they feared that the Somali Government decided to hide the truth about this incident.

Ironically, everybody is afraid of the Somali Military Government, and non was able to even exposed real incidents wherever run by the Somali Military Regime because some thought that they could encounter life imprisonment or the death penalty.

It did not matter whether you were telling false or truce!

One of the third shift nurse on duty said that the nurse who has stolen my baby boy called Istahil. She was one of the senior nurses whom she even suspected eating dead human organs as she once noticed while she has been eating some meat different than animal meat.

Some of the Banadir staff run away, and they said that they never expect to hear such a big crime!

“The nurse said,” “Please be patient.”

I saw her eating some dead human flash!

You can't deny it.”

One of the senior paediatricians cried loudly, oh my God! Is this a false joke? Or are we insane to listen her? “I want to know the truth now,” How did she know? How did she not tell us? And why is she telling us now?

“An old female patient replied,” “My son,” you are still a kid.” Women tell the secrets rarely, and only when someone among them exposed or leaked something to outsiders so, if you know something now then it's enough to make your own decision.

I am deeply sorry to know what is going on? However; it is better to find the criminals before you make us more dirtier than we will be soon. Are we clear to catch the mafia? If so, let's start now before majority of patience know the fact.

*Dr. Badal Kariye*

As of today we learned many crimes but still we did not know the people who committed such crimes at the Banadir Hospital? Please let's seek the plainclothes officer and ask him for further investigations otherwise; nobody will come to this hospital for treatments.

Because everyone would fear to met the mafia nurse who steals babies!.

## Chapter 2

The happy father of the stolen baby who was a ranking Somali government official asked for more help to track down and find his stolen baby boy, and he swore-in to arrest and charge every employee at the Banadir Hospital.

During that time every soldier has had the upper hand to demand and get whatever they wanted because the country was under martial law. Specially, if you were close comrade with the Somali Military Revolution then you were absolutely the best winner of any case.

Every employee scared to face more criminal charges!

“It was very hard for the mother to go through another kind of pain,” “The Somali plainclothes officer was the only lead to find the truth,” “And he could bring the criminal thief into justice.” Could he find the baby stealer?

Or could she forgive the Banadir Hospital employees?

It has not bee easy for a mother to accept loosing a baby boy in the Banadir Hospital which was operated by the Somali Military Government, and she would never tantalize to incriminate all the staff during the 3rd shift.

“She realized the truth,” “Because most of the medical staff knew some disappearance which took place in several occasions at the Disfeer Hospital”. No one ever came forward to know what was going? Well, did the mother take revenge?

“She replied,” All Praise belongs to God!

It is impossible to believe that my child was stolen by a medical staff whose job to save lives however; I believe that everything is possible to happen whether you are very unconscious or conscious even to protect your rights.

I'm afraid so much that my husband would sue everyone then everyone could likely face the death penalty if they did not bring back the stolen baby because it was not a joke to steal the son of a high ranking official within the Somali Military Government.

Gladly, the father of the stolen baby was highly respectful to listen!

Did he get any full incident report from Somali Casa-Balbalare Police Station? Or did he request to file any incident report? “He didn't know the fact that his baby boy was stolen,” “And he thought that everyone was joking with him”.

“He finally cried after he was told the whole truth,” “And he was given an incident police card to track down his case with the Somali Casa-Balbalare Police Station in the near future, and that he could update whether each side got an important information to know the whereabouts of his stolen baby boy.

“The father said,” “He will be willing to find the truth.”

“The mother confirmed,” “She didn't want her husband to fight or charge all innocent employees”. “She replied clearly to his demand for consultations,” What to do with the medical mafia? And she want to punish harshly those who committed this heinous crime.

“She wanted to meet personally with the suspect,” “She requested the Somali plainclothes officer to bring her nearby her bed so, she could ask for what was the main reasons that forced her to steal her baby boy then why she replaced him with someone's dead baby boy from the Banadir Mortuary?

Could she know the truth?

Or she was crying in way we couldn't understand her.

“Demanding the truce mattered a lot to the needy mother who was still in-patient at the Banadir Maternity and Child Health Center.”

How about the cool daddy in the Somali Military Government? It's very clearly that people could change suddenly for some reasons, if and when it relates to emotional disturbance then no predictions about what could happen next?

Unfortunately, if the country is at war then most of the Somali government officials were under constant stress, and it is very common to any society that if and when you are at war to encounter many challenges which would drive simple situations into more complexed ones.

Like it or not!

It's very true that Somalia has been at constant war with the Ethiopian government for the Somali regions which the imperial colonialists gave to Ethiopia in order to make the Somali people confused as they have already done to many other world communities.

Well, if problems don't get solutions then everyone claims until solutions are reached.

However; the father of the stolen baby boy realized that it hasn't been easy for the Banadir Hospital employees to stop criminal accusations till they find the stolen child or they would encounter harsh charges from the Somali Military Government.

No one wanted to see this!

It wasn't a telling history of a comedian!

Or were they able to get away with their crime? Actually, they didn't know how far the Somali Military Government would charge them in the Somali Military Court under marshal law because the country was ruled under marshal law.

And still the babies of the Somali Military Government officials could put you into a dangerous environment where if convicted then you should have to face life-imprisonment or the death penalty. It's your family who escaped more than you.

So, everyone tries to find solutions before they face any military tribunal court!

It's easy and common thing to happy in most of countries where there is a military regime in-charge as well as self-styled bloody dictators so, they must find the stolen baby boy before the head of the country knows that some children are stolen at the public hospitals.

Why did they want to get solutions?

No one knew what could happen next? Surely, the mother of the stolen baby wanted to assure that if the Somali Military Government decided to charge all employees during the 3$^{rd}$ shift then she would preface to let the employees forgiveness.

Rightly, she knew that it wasn't hard for the Somali Military Government to punish more innocent people so, others wouldn't ever dare to steal anything at the Somali Public Facilities in the country and around the globe.

Don't miss with dictators in-charge!

Wisely, she has been a veteran of many challenges before marrying her Somali Government official, and she didn't like to witness him go to the remote areas where there were no enough communications until this case resolved legally.

Additionally, she wanted to get another quick pregnancy too!

So, could her wishes come true? Some of the medical employees wanted her to cool her boss before he would penalize them in the Somali Military Court which most the most feared place to go in and not come back free of crimes even if you were innocent.

Fortunately, there were a few clans whose voice and support had the upper hand than the other clans, and those with the Somali Military Regime had no fear to face, and they could defend themselves in the Somali Military Court.

However; if you're a suspecting anything then possibilities could have been unlimited.

"She wanted easy solutions," "She didn't like to let the Somali Government intervention to deal with this criminal case where her recently born baby boy was till missing". Mainly, she didn't want the medical employees to suffer.

"To her surprise for the truce," "And her husband cool human nature," Then she requested the director of the Banadir Hospital that he has seven days to release the truce about the stolen baby boy, and he could invite the media for press release so, the entire nations knows the truth.

*Dr. Badal Kariye*

It was a demand that hasn't been easy to accept for him!

"And she didn't let him hide the fact from the nation," "She wanted to let everyone in the country know that there were some medical staff who determined to steal babies for many reasons including booming business for smuggling organs as well as selling them to people with impotence.

She needs the stolen child dead or alive!

# Chapter 3

having not been satisfied with such horrible incident, she was very strong to be patient personally, and she let the Somali Authority to find the criminal nurse and bring her into justice. It wasn't funny to loose a new life,

And loosing a newly born baby could have even cost her life however; she has been the even seen cool mother who had experienced many threatening challenges. Considering to her ability in individual patience. She didn't share all information with the father of the stolen baby as to refuel this stressing situation.

“The baby father was a public servant employee with a good outstanding rank in the Somali government where marshal law governs strictly.”

Who dares to expose more truth to him?

I thought that she might even pursuit the criminal nurses and her collaborators harshly but she said clearly that if they tell the truth then she would forgive because she was very pious to believe the divinity.

Doctor! Please you can do your job and take care in-and-out-patients at the hospital until we should get the full reported case of the Somali Police.

Well, the Doctor replied; we would accept your advise and share it with the rest of the employees in order to start our duties, you're a kind mother, and we really thank you. Please I assure you that such crimes won't occur in our hospital thus, we will also notify other local hospitals for vigilance to safeguard & watch children.

I've been a medical doctor since 1960s, and I've never had some suspicious acts in Somalia for children stealing and smuggling but I know the fact today in Somalia. I've never seen someone like how kind & wise you are?

You're a patient heroine to all medical professionals!

“I'll call the Somali plainclothes officers,” “We must ask for his investigations.” Go ahead to sleep!

After while the Somali plainclothes officer arrived with a leading tip, he got exactly the name of the suspicious nurse who knew the whereabouts of the stolen child however; he mentioned that he has fallen in love with her because she is so prettier.

Did the Somali plainclothes man decide to cancel the criminal case? Or was he now handling it in her favor? Usually love drives people to made quicker acts to diverts everything, it looks like now that he was handling in his new lover's favor.

“The Somali Policeman wanted to talk and discourage others not to go after this criminal case,” “He wanted to shut down the reported criminal case”, So, he never felt the pain of the stolen baby's mother, and he thought that he could fool the law.

Could his love turn a pending legal case? Or could he solve anything?

Nicely, the mother of the stolen baby called the plainclothes officer, she gave him that he's no other options than to find the criminal nurse & her collaborators into justice or he'll have face the Somali military law.

The mother added; it is very absurd that the plainclothes officer felt in love with a criminal suspect who has stolen a baby, and talking about her attractions publicly which was unacceptable insanity, It is a good time for Somali authority to intervene governmentally.

Anyway; its is a part of human nature to fall in love with someone or something but if you're dealing with a criminal case then you rather solve it than involving to cover up the crimes which may hurt so many people if they know it.

Mother said; she wanted for some solutions, she'd prefer for further consultations. She was wisely obeying the law while she acknowledged that no one is above the Islamic and customary law in Somalia, and if she can to even take this case into internal tribunal court then she'd have to.

"Well, if he wanted to hide the facts," "Then she'd never know her suspect". Therefore; she snatched his handset walkie-talkie, she alerted all the Somali plainclothes policemen & women who were on this frequency by saying can you hear me? My name is Ms. Mama Jabuti, I want urgent help now!

Who is the Banadir Region Criminal Investigation Department (CID) Commandant? I've someone who has been breaking the law with his own hands, and he doesn't like to do his job so, I want tell you that my newly born child was stolen at the Banadir Hospital. This plainclothes officer was in-charge my case but he is not working properly.

Immediately, one of the highest ranking Somali plainclothes officers replied; go ahead! I copy your voice lady, this is the Bandir Region Criminal Investigation Department (CID) Commandant Hareey, what I can do for you?

Go ahead lady!

The mother said; I've a walkie-talkie handset radio which belongs to a Somali plainclothes officer who was handling a criminal case, and he decided to not expose who has really stolen my child? CID Commandant Hareey, can you help me now?

The CID Commandant Hareey answered; yes, we can help you, where is he now? He seemed to get anger with me then he walked out. And I did not know where he went to? Commandant Hareey, even if he come back to me then I won't talk with him.

I really don't want to die!

The Bandir Region Criminal Investigation Department (CID) Commandant Hareey ordered her to find him and gave back his walkie-talkie, and if he doesn't accept my call then let him know me your location so, I can come to solve your problem. Am I clear dear mother? I mean it!

The mother asked him; are you his superior officer? I need your help because this plainclothes officer has not been doing his job, and he told me clearly that she felt in love with the female nurse who was our targeted suspect for stealing the child.

I'm shocked it! How could he fall in love with a criminal nurse?

What would you do? If someone steals your child, and the authority can do nothing to stop such crimes because they're part of the organized crimes in the country. I know that some of them are not corrupted but the few who corrupted officers gives a bad example for others.

I want my child willy-nilly!

He actually knew that husband was a member of the Somali government officials, I didn't want them to confront in regard to this incident, and he knows what this lunatic plainclothes officers is telling me then we'll have another big problem.

I don't want to witness another disaster in front of my eyes, so please let's solve it.

You must come early CID Commandant!

CID Commandant Hareey said; I'll be there soon. I assure you that we'll document and open a new criminal file for this case until it's completely resolved. We'll get the truth about his findings, and why he didn't arrest her?

As the Banadir Region CID Commandant, I'm not glad listen such unacceptable & misleading acts among the Somali plainclothes officers, and they know that this country is under marshal law. Simply, we need to do something right.

"Be cool if you meet him," "We're on the way".

You're the winner!

And I express my sympathy to what has already happened but we'll try our best to investigate your case and our cheating officer. Generally, mistakes occur however; we always tend to find some solutions to serve the best interest of all.

The mother told to the CID Commandant Hareey that she'd like to easily work with all the Somali concerned authorities for solutions. You're a smart officer! I'm not joking it, I see how you like the job whereby you can deal with cases correctly.

We're going to wait for you so, please be quick, it's getting late, and I want to sleep.

*Dr. Badal Kariye*

I'll send a telegraph message to my husband in order to update this criminal case, and what we should do next? It's very nice to share update information so, we can all work together for better solutions and easy to handle ways in the near future.

We won't like to see more failures from the Somali Police Force!

We've to have solutions to investigate and track down the criminals, please I'll listen to your suggestions but this plainclothes officer may have explain how he is now dealing with case? I want to know it further.

"I can't listen to him, "I don't want to oppose his personal feelings with the criminal nurse". Truly, we need to something.

Ms. Mama Jabuti said; its okay, I can wait for you but you don't need a heavily armed troop to escort and arrest him now in regard to this criminal matter. I called some of my relatives & the husband, they also on the way.

She cried on the walkie-talkie radio, she asked for urgent response before she sleeps. She knew nothing about how corrupted could the Somali military authority hide the facts? She said; hurry up before I sleep.

CID Commandant Harrey replied; I know, it's too late and a bad time to stay outside so, if you want to sleep then you can sleep, we'll come to you tomorrow because we're also tied doing a lot of work today about this case.

The mother replied: it's okay to meet tomorrow, you can start chewing and smoking for relaxation.

CID Commandant Harrey replied: Okay, my dear, we'll meet tomorrow.

# Chapter 4

It was very easy to steal the baby at the hospital and the criminals escaped without detection. It is the responsibility for the Somali security agencies to track down and investigate such heinous acts of intentionally coordinated crime.

Many may ask for help! However; the staff at the hospital were so scared. Well, everyone at hospital prayed for finding the stolen child from their hospital because they feared for martial law, which the Somali Military Regime could impose them.

What loverly thief!

Stealing a child without fear of the medical staff was a big crimes in Somalia, and if found guilt then anyone will have face death penalty. Somalia has had adapted one of the strictest laws for family affairs that was based on the Islamic Creed.

Actually, the mother of the stolen baby has been losing her patience with the Somali security agencies, the medical staff and her families because every time she ask for her baby; they simply replied to her that they were still looking for him.

All she wanted to her baby back to her lap!

"She couldn't listen to lies," "She determined to work with them all the best." Gladly, the father of the stolen bay was very patient and cooperative. He had a charismatic understanding in social ethics and compliance.

Well, it's impossible sometimes to narrate something rightly to worrying person who's has been lacking one of the best gifts in the world, and if you try to convince that you are doing the best to deliver whatever request has been made.

No ways in!

Please I want you to find my child first and foremost!

Go away! Do not come to me if you don't have my baby. I want my stolen child before the Somali Military Regime uses martial law to execute many innocent lives in regard to my stolen child. I mean it clearly.

I know that my child is living with a couple of impotent person!

Don't handcuff the thief before you get my baby because I know that some thieves mayn't show your where they're hiding my baby. Give them whatever they request from you until they hand over my baby to you peacefully.

Okay! We'll do our best to follow your advice until we get your baby. Please if you get any tips or leading information then let's know so, we can use the valuable information to track down the criminal thieves before they steal other babies.

*Dr.Badal Kariye*

I won't give information to other people, and I'll call you as soon as possible whenever I get some valuable information about my baby. Well, if they call me for a ransom then I'll call the nearest police station to report.

Thank you for following the right steps!

"I'm a mother," "And mothers fell more than daddies."

As one of the mothers who miss their babies one way or the other, we've to deal with emotional grievances daily. But we're happy to see our babies whether they're young or grown ups. Mother is a mother!

Already! You're like my mother, and I understand you well now. Please you give us time to do the best because the criminal thugs are smarter than many of our officers in uniform, and as you know that everyone is not working properly nowadays.

We'll take time to further investigate your case!

Surely, this is very interesting for the Somali Police investigators, and they'd carry out complete investigations including doctors and nurses because it looked like an inside job that has been going on at the Banadir Hospital.

We love our police job!

It's fine for me! I want my stolen baby before some people face martial law. Maybe, some of you'll have witness what could happen in the near future in Somalia. Somalia isn't working well nowadays in Somalia so, what's going on? It's up to you!

I don't want to discourage my kids for pursuing medical careers however; I'm scared now because if they realized that their brother has stolen at the Banadir Hospital then they may get angry. It's not good to tell them this criminal case now.

I'll tell them later when they're are all grown ups!

As I'm the Police Officer who's now in-charge this case, I request you not even to mention it to your kids if they're going to school because it may disrupt their school and homeworks. We know kids that are sensitive to issues.

Well, I know that you won't like to see them stressed for this criminal case!

Thank you Officer!

I'll wait for your respond, and I'm very confident that you'll solve this case soon. I know that Police like to solve crimes and arrest criminals however; I think that the thieves can also be Police Officers who have been thieves before they even joined the Somali Police Force.

Don't get angry! "It's my guess."

What clever mother you're!

I think that you know a lot in criminal acts, and you're amazing mother. I couldn't laugh nicely, you shocked me to discuss real issues. After I complete this case then we'll come to learn more about your biography.

You know too much in criminology!

Okay! Go and get my stolen baby!

It's time to sit or sleep till we all get my stolen child, and I know that we're working around the clock for solutions. I'll teach you how to really seek and get the worse criminals such as the ones who had stolen my baby.

I'm only the guardian of my children!

You've been collecting and archiving information about the worse criminals in Somalia, and if you can show me their photos then I'll pick up the photos of those criminals who may steal children in different locations for different reasons.

I can pinpoint criminals who steal children because they've their own characteristics show some facial expressions so, you don't need to use police scary tactics to evaluate criminals. If you want to master such techniques then I'll only teach you after I get my stolen child.

Please do your job!

We're cops, and cops do everything on the job but if they're not following the law then everyone breaks it where crimes happen frequently. This is what's going in Somalia nowadays. We'll try our best to do the job.

Well, bad cops and good cops do their jobs however; the law differentiates among them, and those bad cops will encounter many problematic issues which may lead them for for expulsion from the Somali Police.

I've never been a bad cop since I joined the Somali Police Force in 1960s until now, and there's not been even one case which I couldn't solve it, and I wish to solve your case soon so, let's pray for the best solutions.

My dear mother, please you need to trust the Police!

:I'll trust the Police with all my heart until this case is solved, and I wish you all the best. If you see me angry then I'm not angry with you but I've been angry with the current system of government in Somalia where even my husband can't provide us enough bill.

*Dr. Badal Kariye*

“He works for the government,” “He doesn't get his salary on time.”

Welcome to the reality!

# Chapter 5

I really didn't realize how easy it was to steal a baby from critically ill mother who slept after she delivered the baby. "I think some may like to tease forever." I've never met thieves before so, I really didn't know why they targeted me? "I'm a victim."

Surely, thugs do everything nowadays however; as the world develops more clearer police investigation for forensics then it'd be easier to track them down because it's very normal for criminals to leave some kind of evidence behind related them to any crimes.

I know it so, you can collect some evidences!

Mother! Have you been working with the police? I'm truly surprised how deeply you have learned the police activities? As I'm Police Officer, I'm still learning it so, please if you served the police before then let me know because I want to learn easily how you mastered for the information gathering.

:"I want to become the criminal analyst."

Okay! Son, in this world where you live, you'll always encounter surprises so, if you're eager to know and learn then most people are very compassionate to share and teach you their experiences if you're not idiot.

So, accepting bribes will always degrade your reputation!

Mother! I accepted your advise however; I'm still learning to achieve my goals in the Somali Police Force. As we know that Somali Police is still one of the best and multilingual police force which many countries in the world decided to come and get training at the Somali Police Academy literally known as Escola Policia.

If and after you train me then I won't tell or share your experience in covert operation because I understood that you didn't want to share more know however; I'll come back soon after I complete my duty on the job.

I'll be happy to meet you later in this week!

Well, my baby is missing, the Somali Police are searching him so, I may try to organize a grassroots campaign for search and rescue operations in the nation wide therefore; we can easily notify everyone in the nation to report even if they see suspicious persons.

Every mother should feel the pain!

I feel this pain every second!

I do not actually know what the Somali Military Government will do if such thug are caught by the Somali National Security Services or the Somali Police. Unfortunately, they'll face life imprisonment or the death penalty.

As they said before: Roma wasn't built in a day!

Let's work together for better security in Somalia and the world because thieves are part of every society. Some may do silly things which we can't even guess but we can talk about it whenever they do it.

I can try my best to locate possible suspects by tomorrow.

Well, I' call you tomorrow with some updates. Let me go to my office at the Somali Police Headquarters, and I'll also give your case information to traffic officers on the job for search the stolen child.

I appreciated your input well!

What lovely mother you're! "I wish to be your son in law in the near future," Please! I want you to tell your daughters that you've met a good and honest many within the Somali Police Force. Maybe, one of them can say, who is he?

And I want that one to be my wife in the near future.

Clearly, I'm lucky man!

Officer! Well, I'll tell them to your name and where you're currently working at? If one of my daughters ask for you or even mention to interest in you then I'll definitely contact you with the information and her requirements.

I know that some low rank officers are still fighting for good pay however; every marriage comes with its own richness, in this case, don't be my guest. We're living in world where the strong tries to survive mostly.

My dear son, don't worry! If you've no money then I'll still try my best to cover up some of the shopping coasts for your future, that is my daughter Najmo! Because she loves to marry a man who works for the nation.

And when I reach home tonight then I'd inform her that I met an officer who is searching my stolen child.

Wow! Thank you mother!

Don't mention it!

"I'm very confident," "You'll soon be my son in law."

We'll also be good neighbors too! I mean it. Excuse me! Are your parents still alive? Do you live in Mogadishu? I want to meet them.

Please you can arrange our meeting if and whenever you've time to do so.

Okay! My future mother in law, we'll do the best. I'm late now, I get to go so, I'll call you later after I leave the office. What's best time to call you? Can I call you at 9:00 PM? Maybe, it's good time for family to listen to my voice.

Surely, I'll call you.

It was very nice to meet you and know more about you.

Please! If you call me later this evening then you'll have tell whoever picks up the ringing telephone that you're a Police Officer who's working on my case then you can ask for where is your mother? Maybe, if I'm sleeping then he or she'll wake me up.

By the way, I'll tell my children who you are? So, please you can continue your official duties.

It's so sad that many mothers cry whenever their children are stolen, and it's an universal crime which increases annually however; child sexy and pornography strives globally while police aren't trying to investigate and charge criminals.

I want all the international organizations for police and secret services to work together for good governance in the world where innocent children are kept safely and harmoniously than in ugly and awkward environment.

Children are  the true flowers of this world, and their safety should be priority number locally, regionally and worldly. I think many NGOS and international organizations acting on behalf of the children aren't openly telling the truth.

So, I must start and engage a global champaign to end child labor, slavery and sex.

If many people join me then I'll simply share my vision for our future generations. I want to welcome all inspiring people on board so, we can address such heinous acts within every corner even though some more populous countries do the most worse acts in child labor, slavery and sex.

If I need some donations then I'll ask for it later. I want my fellow world citizens to campaign for children rights because every child has the right to get and access his basic rights than talking and employing him or her into the world of dangerous acts such child labor, slavery and sex.

It's mot a good way of living in a word where our children face child labor, slavery and sex under age, and it's our responsible to act and enact laws which govern for the betterment of children and disabled people in every nation on this earth.

My best try is only to get back the stolen child but I want every mother to feel safer than fearing to lose a child under these circumstances for the child labor, slavery and sex. I'll level my ability to their interests.

*Dr. Badal Kariye*

So, if you're interesting in my campaign then you can join us in the future.

I love children!

# Chapter 6

Having been unsatisfied with on-going criminal activities in the country, I decided to leave Somalia whenever I found my stolen child. It's only child who has been encouraging to stay and live in Somalia although I want to study in abroad.

I love embroidery and doing my own professional things!

I learn how to sew and make embroidery items with intention to stay away from government service or other politically related agendas in Somalia because it was very hard to trust someone during the Somali Military Regime.

It wasn't easy to earn money if you're living in a city where you've not diverse population so, this was the reason I moved into the capital of the Republic of Somalia. I met someone who completely changed my way of learning for public services.

I always thank her forever! Dulmar!

She's been changing the lives of many people like me through vocational education at her home nearby Sigale Market, Hodan Distirict, Mogadishu City. She was one of the women who encouraged me to marry and take care of my family personally.

As I'm still missing my child, I always remember my ex- teacher's advice which wasn't to trust the Somali Military Regions and its operating facilities in the country because there were many untold stories taking place in the country.

I didn't understand her advise!

I understand it now but I can't do something right.

I've been working for many years to help my family and survive however; I encountered this crime at public hospital so, I mayn't tell you why the thief stolen my child? Perhaps, there is someone who want to punish me emotionally.

Maybe, it is set up!

If I don't obey the interests of the unknown people then it's also a danger to my family. Somalia has been heading to wrong directions, and I wished to find my child before everything collapses and disintegrates.

I remembered a catholic nun saying that there were many issues going on at the Banadir Hospital, and I should be careful in the future because she couldn't trust the Hospital and its personnel who've been working for third party interests.

She said: it's hard to believe what was going in Somalia?

God knows who stolen my baby!

*Dr. Badal Kariye*

I didn't know how this hospital has been operating, and I'm deeply astonishing your input what's going on? I want to learn it more from you so, would you mind to tell me more? Or are you're willing to share it with the Somali press?

Dear Nun, we must exposed such secret to the public wisely.

I mean it!

Generally, speaking to tell the truth may lead us into more danger however; we're only trying to save mothers and children so, if you know something that it's illegal acts within the Banadir Hospital then let's fizzle it out.

We know that many people may worry to know the facts, and understanding will take time in the general public as opinion grows among the people. People must know such crimes happens daily at the hospitals in Somalia and around the world.

I'm not expert for information!

I know that many nuns are practicing Christians however; this is one of the Islamic countries so, why did you come? Were you coming to confer us? Please let me tell you that we're naturally converted to Islam when it reached us in centuries ago.

I want tell you that you're wasting time and money, and the majority of people won't listen to your infidel propagation so, you better understand it now though we're only sharing what's the best interests to the general public?

You know it!

"The Nun said," "We're all trying the best in lifestyle and faith," "If you want to change your lifestyle," "Then, "It's all okay."

It's not wise to change your faith, and you've already cleared for me that. What piety! You're definitely religious. Does Islam teach you Christianity? What do you believe about Christianity? Do you know Jesus?

I simply relied to her: I knew that you're a catholic nun, and it's very clear to me that you can't tell me to believe a human being as a son of God! So, if you want to live in Somalia peacefully then you shouldn't interfere with religious propagation in Somalia.

Jesus is one of the God's prophets, and he was a son of virgin Mary. As I read the Holy Qur'aan then it mentions him clearly that he was one of the prophets descended to mankind for a guidance to the right path.

Well, those who truly believed Jesus as a prophet then they really know that Jesus said and even mentioned in the Holy Gospel that there'd be another prophet after him named Mohamed so, who messed up this truth out of the Holy Gospel?

Making changing in any holy scripture was, is and will always be a big sin, and Allah will punish those who did it intentionally to confuse people and let the demons misguide people from the right path to the wrong path where hell will be your home forever.

I'm not easy person to accept lies!

The Nun said: Alright! Please don't share our conversation. I'm really scared the way you've spoken to me clearly. Somalis don't like to talk or convert into other faiths even if he or she is ignorant, well, it's a societal vision.

I tried to share mission with you, and I offered to work with you anyhow; you turned down my offer so that you don't want to even listen it. I understood your point straight forward, and I respected it. I want to meet you by tomorrow if you've time.

We'd visit my office!

You'd be see many Somalis too!

Lady! I'm not interesting in this visiting offer so, you can leave me alone now. You can go ahead wherever you;d be going to. I want cook some food for my children, and you wasted me time talking about Jesus which I don't know. We, the Muslim world call him Prophet Essa!

You know nothing but lies which were taught by the philosophical theologians who had been contradicting each for many centuries, and if you want to learn something correctly then you need to buy the Islamic Holy Scripture or the Holy Qur'aan.

Please you better read the Holy Qur'aan!

It mentions all prophets and narrates their histories well, and this is a clear sign for the mankind to know the facts whether you're Muslim, Christian or believe in other faiths which aren't based on monotheistic religions.

As many people change their way of lifestyle then I'm not one of the susceptible to convert so, I wished her the best. I knew that she's has been trying to convert Somalis women which her mission was really based on.

She me the wrong person!

I love Allah! You want me to love a person like me with your lies! As you're a catholic nun, it's wise for me to listen your missing acts and believe in Islam so, you've already failed my personal scrutiny in your own Christianity.

I read a lot to know more facts and news around the world. So, if you want to convert to Islam then I'll be very glad to welcome you as my sister in Islam thereby; we can share everything. Does it possible to convert? If no, then Goodbye!

*Dr.Badal Kariye*

No, I'll be converting to Islam in the near future, and goodbye too.

# Chapter 7

It's very physiological punishment to lose of your newborn baby who's has been stolen by unknown thugs. I wanted to enjoy after his delivery because he was my youngest child. I love him so much. It's still easy to accept facts.

On my way to home I met with a butcher driving donkey cart who offered me a ride which I couldn't turned away. I accepted his offer then he asked for me if I was still a virgin girl who's looking for a man.

Unfortunately, I didn't want to tell my problem.

He was so interesting in marriage!

"I told him that I was married lady," "And my husband is working as public servant." Hardly, he said to me; is your husband working for the governance? I noticed that I I said yes, then he could let me get off from his donkey cart.

Even he was shaking badly.

I mightn't tell him then I've not done wrong. It wasn't easy talk after he's known that my husband works for the public services. I laughed at him, and he said to me; why are you laughing at me? I'm not laughing at you.

I laughed how arrogant we've been asking for questions when I've been emotionally and physically tied. If you're not helping me to silence and a good ride to reach my final destination then let me get off.

Someone has stolen my newborn!

Oh1 lady, get off my donkey cart now!

I'm not interesting to help you from now because if you're not acting normally. I didn't know that you've been seeking a stolen baby. I heard such stories many time during last decade in Somalia maybe, there is a business for black market.

It's something going on in the world!

I'm still seeking my stolen newborn baby so, if you see someone announcing it clearly that they see or they have a newborn baby boy then let's know because I can give my contact. It's possible to see because you're working at butchery market.

Many changes exits in this changing wold!

Lady! I'll drop you off this area if you can walk now.

Thank you tell me the truth!

You're not joking mother, you really surprised me to know more facts about Somalia. There is not a functioning government but a bunch of thugs with military uniforms. We're fed up with these uniformed soldiers collecting taxes everyday.

It's not good to trust police or uniformed thugs in Somalia.

I get to go now so, please get off my donkey cart!

It's not to use common sense when you know all thugs do the same and apply for laws against you if you don't buy them bribes well everyday. These uniformed men collect our taxations but when we ask them to build good roads then they only laugh at us.

Truly, we've to work together and stop corruptions if not then you need to get off my donkey cart now, I don't want to get involve problems. I was arrested once for a minor issue then I met many innocent people at the $20^{th}$ Jail.

Be careful!

Well, some told me about another worse jail in Mogadishu which they called it Godka literally meaning the Hole Prison in Mogadishu City. So, I can't tolerate to see another problem where I'd lose my donkey cart and butcher license.

It's very easy to encounter problems if you don't bribe them because they can make you a criminal case against you then they'd arrest you which may cost you to stay in behind prison the rest of your life so, no one dares to object their demands.

I don't want to lose my butcher license.

Okay! Donkey cart driver, I'd not like to jeopardize your job.

I actually didn't understand a lot before but there were many crimes which people within the government commits, and no one talks about it directly. So, if I can't help people then how should people help to find my newborn?

After I get my newborn baby then I'll try to send my best wishes to the People and the Republic of Somalia. I'll encourage them to work together for common cause rather than destroying their nation smoothly.

Because if some people act above the law of the land then it's your responsible to stop criminals within.

Don't be silly!

It wasn't a simple ride with you, and I appreciated your input for matters which are currently taking place in Somalia which the government is the doer of every wrong move, and it'll crash soon as hoax as liars bleed to consciousness.

Be careful!

I see shallow waters in public roads everyone, and people think that its very normal but when we plunge into more dangerous issues. I think that we need to hire professional engineers who could stop more entrenching matters in Somalia.

Only Allah can save Somalia now!

There are a lot of things which I didn't appreciate however; if and when you're weak then it's possible to encounter many problems. Well, you've heard that the government planned to execute more shakes for exposing fact and stopping the illegal move of the Office of the President.

This should be one of the reminding illegal move if the government executes the Sheikhs for telling the truth.

Hey! Lady, I don't want to hear this matter!

Seriously, everything is going crazy, and this is the beginning of troubling and collapsing government in Somalia. "I saw crazy acts," "I've never seen people dying for the truth." "God will reward them in the hereafter life."

Donkey cart driver, don't tell or share such conversations against the Somali Military Regime because some people may trade you in order to get name or ranks from this corrupted government. You're luck man!

"I'm not fond of this corrupted military dictatorship."

If this military regime is worse than devil if they kill the Somali Sheiks who exposed their lies because the religion is Islam, and no one can change the Holy Qur'aan because Allah said clearly that Allah will always protect it from anything until the doomsday.

Please I don't know that you've kids so, don't let them to hear what's going on in Somalia nowadays? I wish you all the best for helping the ride. I earned your trues to know more about people who've been working at market, and some their views are alarming.

I wish you to work hard and bring up your children in a good mood.

Bye!

Bye old lady!

Goodbye donkey cart driver and butcher! It was very nice to meet you, and I'd always remember your advice. I love my country but the wrong people have been operating it illegally after they occupied power on October 21st in 1969 with bloodless coup d'etat.

*Dr. Badal Kariye*

Assassinating President his Excellency Abdirashid Ali Sharmake was a big mistake for those who did it intentionally and politically, and most of them are still in trouble one way or the other. Somalia is at war with its own people.

# Chapter 8

Not still believing that there are many illegal crimes going on in the world for children kidnapping and its smuggling for black market organs. I understood very clear that it's a kind of business which works in every country around the world.

It wasn't good news to know such crimes are also going on in Somalia!

I met some experts to work for my case to work as private detectives because I couldn't trust the Somali Security Services. They're as corrupted as the smuggler and other criminals in the world. I'd rather hire private detective in abroad.

Remembering many crimes in which took place in Somali since 1960s until now, many a majority of the Somali people are fed up with the Somali Military Regime. We've been witnessing many failures in every job within Somalia.

I'm a witnessing victim too!

Crimes are crimes, and there is no one above the law however; I can tell you that the Somali Military Regime has been acting above the law though the Somali Military Government made significant change and development for providing free health and education.

"I'd not outspoken it clearly."

Evading my vision wasn't enough however; people weren't able to understand what was going in Somalia? And it could lead us into anarchic war that might last for many years in the near future if we'd not stop all criminals.

It's not also wise to weak a big shirt than your body!

I couldn't stop silly con men who've been wasting my time for finding the stolen baby, and everyone was indirectly asking for bribes. This was the reason that forced me to hire private detectives in abroad so, they could early investigate my case.

However; it was very tough to hire private detectives in abroad, and I hired them fortunately then I'd have had challenges to bring them into Somalia because the Somali Military Regime could take it into another spying work in Somalia.

It's hard to hire!

As I tried my application for a private detectives then I was told to come and meet the Director of the Somali National Security Services. I was shocked to know that someone has already inform to the Somali National Security that I'd the intention to hire private foreign detectives.

I'd not go there!

I didn't contact to the Director of the Somali National Security Services.

It wasn't easy for me to understand who notified my intentions to the Director of the Somali National Security Services? Well, I noticed that even every house in Somalia, there is someone who's been working with he Somali National Security Services.

I want to go the countryside!

I bagged my stuff and notified my children that I was planning to visit the countryside so, I could get some fresh scent and sights. It's obvious to leave condensed urban areas so, you'll fee rejuvenated and emotionally well.

My husband won't be willing to accept this travel!

I love the countryside, it's very nice!

I want to go and invite all media houses so, I can tell and share my story. It's encouraging to share exactly what's going on in Somalia? I'm still feeling the pain, I want to forget it in the countryside until I get good news.

My husband came, and he saw our bagged stuff at the living room. He asked me; where are you going to? What's up? Are you going to abroad? I'm astonished to see these bagged stuff! Are you going with the children?

Yes, my children and I are going to visit the countryside!

If you want to travel with us, you're welcome!

Alright! I'm coming with you, let me bag my stuff.

I called the Bus Service Company for reserving our tickets. I wanted my mother to accompany with us to countryside. I love my mother, she knows too much about the countryside so, she could help us navigate through our sojourn.

It's very nice to go together!

Gladly, we got enough tickets from the Bus Service Company. We're ready to travel by Monday so, I called my children's Qur'anic School Teacher whom I personally informed that my children and I were traveling to the countryside for 3 months.

I also called to my children's secular schools to know that we're traveling to the countryside for 3 months. I want everyone to know that we'll be away for awhile. I've not been arranging this travel however; it's my interest to take some vocation.

I need it! And my children must accompany me because they'd not get someone to take care if I left them at home. It's my will to see our countryside with children so, they'd like it more in the future for their vocation.

We met Somalia's comedian on our way to the countryside, and he asked my husband where we were going to? My husband told him that we're on vocation to visit the countryside then the comedian asked him again which countryside are you heading to?

My husband was surprised why did this comedian want to know us in details? "He asked the comedian," "Are you not a comedian Dulwade? Or you're not Dulwade! Have you ever working for the Somali Military Regime?

Surely, everyone works for the Somali Military Government, Mr. Traveler!

My children and I are traveling to Lego town where Somali people go and enjoy for their vocations, and I'm off duty so, I didn't understand why you asking me for hard questions? I love my country than this brutal military regime.

So, if you want to report something rightly then you can do the best. We're not playing games, and let's relax and have smooth ride on this bus. I know that you're trying to report false allegations which have not fruitful outcome.

Please you better be a good service man!

Okay! I want to tell you that I'd be riding on this bus with you, I was told to follow you to the countryside because the Somali National Security Service thought that you've been planing to travel to abroad.

I know clearly that there are many suspicious cases against you, Mr. Traveler! We're watching you everyday because we'd not like to see you joining the rebellious faction which have been opposing the existence and the rule of the Somali Military Regime.

We know that someone has stolen your child at the Banadir Hospital, and we're still working on your crimes. I wish that the other department of the Somali Security Agencies should soon solve it for you. If you want to know my name.

It's true that you called my name correctly, I'm Dulwade! Dulwade is literally meaning "On-rider."

You're welcome!

I knew your name, Mr. Dulwade! I wasn't interesting in to join with the Somali Security Agencies however; I know all plainclothes and intelligence officers who've been working in Mogadishu City since 1960s until now.

Unfortunately, I didn't understand why was the Somali Military Regime to keep an eye on me? I'm not a rebel, and I don't want to join them. My children, wife and I are traveling to visit the countryside and spend our vocation in the green lands where animals and people can enjoy tranquilly and freshly.

Have nice day Mr. Dulwade!  We understood you well.

## Chapter 9

Forgiving the criminals who stolen my newborn and relying on what's best for me in the future was key interesting and expecting more gains than my loss. It's good to forgive sometimes so, the bad omen shouldn't affect you badly.

I wasn't sure how it'd take to seek my stolen child!

Returning from the countryside my family and I met an old lady on the way who was Italian Somali visiting the countryside, and I told her that we visited the countryside for a vocation and tranquility then she laughed at me.

Do you want to visit Italy? It's very nice!

I replied no! Italy is the center of the Christianity! "That is why I'm not interesting to visit."

So, many crimes occur over there!

No! Italy is same as other countries in the world, same as Somalia! You misunderstood my store about Italy. I know that you can also hire the best private detectives in the world, we call them the Italian Carabinieri.

So, if you're interesting in to hire detectives from the Italian Carabinieri then my brother works there, I can tell him to contact your family when I go back to Italy. I truly don't like the crimes which are nowadays going in Somalia.

I let you my offer so, don't be my guest!

I thank you for your offer, I know that the Somali Security Services played key roles not only for investigations here in Somalia but also in abroad, they're very successful to detect and investigate high profile cases of corruption in Europe.

So, if you didn't know it then you might read it through many European newspapers and magazines. I'm very proud to have here in Somalia some of the best investigative detectives in the world who can pinpoint crimes easily.

If you'd like to send your brother for three month course then you're welcome! Because if he arrives in Somalia for a police internship then they'll offer some apprenticeship. He'll learn a lot in criminology, which he hasn't ever tried before.

I'll hire him if he take such courses in Somalia.

He'll learn new fields of criminology in Somalia, and its only unique to Agricultural, pastoral and nomadic communities. It's called agricultural, pastoral and nomadic criminology.

I want to offer him something new in Somalia!

Well, you know it that there's no school in the world which teaches agricultural, pastoral and nomadic criminology. We've such a police training school in Somalia, and many countries around the world came to learn it.

So, it's only western world to offer everything!

I don't know how long it'll take for me to find my stolen child?

Oh! Are you a policewoman? You know a lot about the Police! Maybe, you've had some training in the Somali Police Force. Please I was truly surprised to know how you simply explained it, and how you're clear about their activities.

You must be working in the market!

As you know that many countries in the world differs, and the Police do the best to decrease crimes in each and every country however; some countries are nowadays adapting modernized scientific techniques for crime laboratory and analysis.

You're knowing too much!

I'll ask for my brother if he could ship some of old fashion police equipments to the Somali Police Force. If you want to accept this shipment, and you can distribute the police equipments to every police station's which needs it.

Are you ready to know it?

No, I'm not a policewoman! I really understood you that you're not a tourist. You're an intelligence agent so, are you working with the Italy? Or are you working as double agent? I'm fortunately eager to know it now.

You're trying to recruit special contacts in Somalia!

I won't be one of your special contacts in Somalia however; you can send your brother to Somalia for extra learning in agricultural, pastoral and nomadic criminology because we've the best school in criminology of such above-mentioned fields.

You're not welcome to Somalia if some of the current authorities in power know your ugly mission in Somalia. We don't like Italians and British for separating Somalis into five sections before they left us in 1960s after we forced them to leave Somalia in war and peace.

No! Madam, I came to Somalia for tourism, I'm not working with spy agency. This is my contact card!

I don't need your contact card, you can write whatever you want on it. If you're working spy agency then what made you to make more spy offers to me? I know, who you're? Please leave me alone now!

Once upon time you've been working with spy agency, it's true that you're actively working with spy agency now however; you're seeking a vital information to sell so, I won't be a bait for that! You better know it well!

I love my country!

"I'm not a traitor," "It was a nice day to meet you on this bus."

I want you to know that there were four Somali National Security Services Officers on this bus, and they've been recording and collecting information about your close contacts in Somalia since you'd arrived in Somalia and until now we're still on this bus.

It's possible for them to stop and ask for more questions later when we get off this bus.

Please it's my advice to leave Somalia, and I want you to tell your Italian Government that they can't no longer fool us into more trouble. Somalis know the painful slavery which the Italian colony carried out in Somalia so, we're still feeling it.

By the way, if you want to offer me some detectives to come in Somalia for investigating my case then they'd first apply for entry visa from the Somali Ministry of Foreign Affairs which can or can't grant entry visa to Somalia.

I know that he'll follow the normal procedure to apply for entry visa!

Dear Madam, I don't want any trouble in Somalia, I'm not here for trouble, and only I want is to learn and know people in Somalia. This is my fourth visiting to Somalia since 1960s so, I want to help you then you can help my brother in turn.

If that isn't okay then I won' border you again.

Hello! Ms. White! I'm not interesting in your offer, you're genuinely clever to influence people however; it's working it with me. I mean that we're not on the right path for understanding negotiations. Would you like to visit Somalia another day?

If you'll visit Somalia another time then please don't come with nuns because I met one of the Catholic Nun in Somalia who's been acting very suspicious and working as spy agent after I've manipulated her under cover operations in Somalia.

"She wasn't a good actress in espionage," "I noticed her first question."

Well! If you're not a policewoman then who trained you well in criminology? You surprised me extraordinarily how you've learning in criminology? I love you! I appreciated it well! I'll leave by tomorrow night to Rome, Italy.

I thank you for your information and offer, I wasn't interesting it. If you'll visit Somalia in the near future then don't ask for silly questions to recruit people illegally. Goodbye!

# Chapter 10

life hasn't been easy nowadays in this changing world where few rich people had been trying to control the local, global and international finance to dominate and colonize us indirectly and mentally. I learned a lot before now!

Well, comparing this challenge to my problem, it's possible for us to not detect what crooked policymakers are doing to mislead and colonize us. There are some people who think twice, and my reject their dirty policy.

I mean, wake up world citizens!

As you listen to world media, did you hear many international organizations planing to reduce world population growth? I sometimes asked myself where are these organizations made for? If we all know that they're not helpful to control the growth world population.

They only create further medical crisis which they then seek for medical treatments so, their pharmaceutical companies prosper from the medical disasters which they have experimented in places around the world where innocent people suffer from it.

We must stop such heinous medical practices in the world!

I didn't want to vaccinate my children!

And I don't believe it doing vaccinations!

Surely, I thought that I couldn't understand how they worked in many places but it's money which they let corrupted officials for a license to operate and commit more medical crimes in any country which they import their medicine for sale.

I know that some of these world companies are doing their health related businesses truly, however; eager market competitions drives them to even not following safety regulations and standards in many countries around the world including so-called advanced nations.

We need to stop their medical damages!

Wake up world citizens!

If you want my help then let's seek my newborn before they use him for medical experiment or harvest his organs. It's happening in the world! This is one of the serious businesses which even many international law enforcement are still fighting.

I called one of the Somali Police investigators who's been handling my case, and I asked him if he got any leads. "He replied to me; we're still working on it! If we get any information the we'll let you know it before we store it.

Be safe!

I said okay! I'll be waiting for your call officer. “I'm so worried,” “I love to find my child.” I know that you're doing the best job. I knew one thing clear, you couldn't argue with a Somali Crime investigators because they could put me into trouble.

It's easy for them to fabricate a crimes, and they blame you that crimes. If you couldn't say and smile to them then they might think that you're not respecting them. Am I one step ahead? Yes, I was one step ahead.

Be smart in this world!

You're friends may act the enemies for money!

I mastered not fear for telling the truth even if they wanted me dead! I liked to share my personal and political views, and maybe, this was one of the reasons which the unknown thug had stolen my newborn.

I don't want to die for saying something which the current military regime didn't like it anyhow; I needed to keep quiet until they find my stolen newborn baby. I'd not option to accept or disagree with the Somali crime investigators.

This is now working smoothly!

It's not wise for us to come outside and say, what you're doing in the country is wrong? If you dared it to say publicly then they could even arrange you for the death penalty as they did to innocent Sheiks who rejected their gruesome crimes in Somalia.

I couldn't leave Somalia!

Well, have you ever heard how many people died for saying something politically agitating the Somali Military Regime? Or how many people are now in prison? We all know it clearly so, I must only ask for if they find any information about my stolen child.

I only want my kid!

A couple of years ago I met an old French women who narrated me that she'd learned the social and political ethics of the world population through her traveling adventures however; she couldn't understand about Somalis well!

And she was planning to come and write a book about the Horn of Africa countries. I was surprised her interests in Somalia. She told me that Somalia was, is and will be the connecting trade hub in the near future.

She said to me; I want you to know that we, the Western world are now fighting against communism so, after we won then many of the western countries are bound to invest Somalia which is located the best place in the Horn of Africa strategically.

So, you can give birth more babies to defend Somalia!

As the French colonized part of Somalia which is now called Djibouti, we're still trying to investigate only where we firstly colonized but the rest of Somalia and in the Horn of Africa so, if you want to work with me then let me know.

"I'm billionaire who wants to investigate in the Horn of Africa," "It's very important to us," "And you can be our contact and contractor within the Somali Military Government." If you accept offer then you'll be shareholder.

I welcome to my company!

And if you know that another person who's interesting in such offer, please share it. You're strong business lady, you seemed to me that you've your own businesses in Mogadishu. Please welcome on board!

Hello! "I'm not a traitor," "I love Somalia."

If you want to invest in Somalia then there is a functioning regimes in Somalia so, if you've some business investment to Somalia then please you can go to the Somali Chamber of Commerce or you can visit the Somali Ministry of Finance.

They'll tell you more options for investments in Somalia!

If you're a businesswoman then you're fine to invest Africa. It's too complicated to share resourceful ideas about investments in Africa however; you're now targeting the best place, and we'll see how far it will convince you to invest Somalia.

You better careful investing in the security sectors! Thank you very much for understanding my advice, You'll consider it well.

I thanked you wholeheartedly! I won't invest until I read all the investment procedures and regulations. I really don't want to go back to Europe because I love the warm calamity which fits my living hobby so, would you mind?

No, I don't mind!

Which district is the best to live in? Which district is the best to open business in Mogadishu City? I'll follow up your guidance advice. I love Somalia too! That is why I came here! I'm not spy agent so, please you don't have to guess me wrongfully.

Good luck French investor! I want to go to the Hodan District Police Station where I'd ask for some information about my newborn so, goodbye!

*Dr. Badal Kariye*

I walked straight along the Dadka road in Mogadishu City until I reached the Somali Traffic Police Headquarters literally known 888 where I fell down on the ground for few minutes then I got a ride to my home.

I couldn't reach the Hodan District Police Station!

# Chapter 11

Perfecting my search for the stolen newborn boy, I encountered many challenges and injustice within the Somali Criminal Justice where if you said something rightly about the various on-going criminal injustice.

Then you;ll end up in a jail!

I'd my faith to search my stolen kid, and when I find him then my family and I were ready to move out and resettle abroad so, we couldn't be victims of these on-going criminal injustice in Somalia and Africa at large.

I got a visa invitation many times before, I told my inviter that I wasn't ready to leave Somalia because it's the place to live in and work by all means however; I never assumed that it'd force me to leave voluntarily.

I'll try my best to work hardly!

As I was also inspiring artist! "I couldn't share my arts," "And they'd often say that my arts are opposing developments in the countryside." I mightn't share my information because I didn't want the crooked crime investigators to incriminate me.

I knew that they could do harm without trace!

I want everyone to know that we must protect our children because we can't even trust in hospitals and schools as many thugs turned to smuggle kids out of the country for many reasons while some corrupted cops are letting them to get away with their crimes.

We know that money is so powerful key to open and influence hunger stomach to double cross the law and commit acts of criminal insanity. After all, we must blame innocent cops when we couldn't stop the acts of crooked cops in the world.

I wasn't happy to know all facts!

We'll be trying to talk and blame only because cops are strong, and they work for another corrupted government led by a military regime which thinks that they're the only guardians of everything while they commit many crimes in the country.

Positively, the Somali Military Government built educational sectors and health with the assistance of the Somali people however; we only give them a credit for coordination of the developed sectors but they're as corrupted as the devil itself.

It's true!

Many wouldn't like to listen truth yet, and there'd be a time when everyone bursts the anger and start retaliating acts of no solutions to internal crisis.

*Dr. Badal Kariye*

Many internal crisis are refueling and heading us to civil war in the near future if injustice practices are continuously prospering while a majority of peace are suffering from hunger and illnesses which can be cured.

I saw many crimes which have been going on in the country, and if you dared to expose it then they could blame you as a traitor so, they'd cover up their illegal acts so, who to trust was questionable task? And I didn't like it.

As we know the facts, the Somali Military Regime is above the constitution!

I couldn't mess with up!

Acting as a low grade person could only give me an opportunity to seek my stolen baby boy with the criminally insane regime while my life wasn't in a danger of their rotating acts of military suffocations and intimidations.

If you want to know how I was feeling as a mother, and how I knew that some acts in the country were going on then you'd really appreciate it my tranquility for dealing with such challenging contra problems.

I advised myself to rely on my visionary mission!

Please if you come to encounter such crimes somewhere in the world then don't first rush to inform cops because they may be corrupted too. Take time to investigate and analyze your information before you let someone know it.

It could harm you if you said something that wasn't right! I was having many challenges in my country, and everyone acts as a spying informant because they didn't do it then they knew that we're not able to expose all.

I can't run away!

I'd only run away if I get back my stolen kid, and I don't know how long it'll take to find him? I'm so shocked. I've never been scared in such crimes going on in Somalia before but I'm nowadays feeling it painfully.

No constitution! Except martial law which was based on October 21, 1961, and everyone decided to silence because nobody wants to face bogus charges which could cost their lives. There were jokes in Somalia!

Martial Law was the consciousness of failing and threatening law in the country!

All I cared for was my stolen kid, and I planned to resettle my children to abroad. I've no money in spite of my willing, I knew that everyone should help me but I was so scared to inform my plan to abroad.

Because the Somali Military Government didn't like people to travel abroad!

Well, I loved my country but they wanted me to leave so, they could grab my assets. It's out of control! They haven't been working legally, and I couldn't bribe everyone within the government so, it was a nice decision to leave Somalia.

I wanted my children to get good education and live in safer country!

Undoubtedly, I seemed as a challenger to many but I was only a mother in trouble. I'd felt more like paranoid than their shits. As you can try the best out of their dark holes where they abused innocents who opposed the martial law.

I walked in offices where everyone wanted to get bribery so, they could give me information about the my stolen kid. I was a friend to all who offered me some information while I wasn't a friend with cops asking for bribes.

You can't break my heart!

As I wasn't interesting to offer bribes then I knew that my case should drag out for some time. Politely, I've to offer some bribes to get important information about my case from the Hodan Police Station before I got our passports.

Even if you apply for a passport then it's obvious that the Somali Military Regime would ask for more questions which they'd even deny it if they say it that you're escaping away from their internal crimes in the country.

I'm not fond of it!

We're all fed up to work with the Somali Military Regime!

I've never had a chance to meet the commander of the Somali Military Regime so, I always listen to him on the radio and television, and he's been acting above the law because he brought and based on this county what I called; the deceitful martial law!

We don't want martial law so, he must hold elections and return the rule to civilian hand soon. I heard that there were ethnic cleansing going on in some regions, and no one talked about it because everyone was scared.

I didn't accept crimes!

I told many of my close friends why I didn't like the military rule in the country was one thing, I loved democracy for all. I'm now ready to fight for a democracy before it gets more dirtier fears in the country.

I can't find my stolen kid! Lastly, everyone knows the rule of law in the country! “I won't talk nonsense until I get back my stolen newborn.”

# Chapter 12

I was told that my brother who's been living at Dagahbur, Somali region in Ethiopia was very sick, and his children were confused and fled from Dagabur. Then I couldn't know what to do because this was another problem.

I'd not option to stay in Mogadishu City!

I bought a lorry ticket to Ethiopia!

I've never told my plans to anyone, and I wasn't happy to leave however; I'd not option to contemplate because my brother was so important, and I used to please and enjoy his joyful talks. I brought up him to look after our animals.

Increasingly, I don't like problems but if you encounter it then there are solutions to it. It's possible for me to think and get advice from my family. I wasn't glad to mislead or misunderstand me because I want everyone to be happy.

I boarded on the UD lorry to Ethiopia!

On my way to the border between Somalia and Ethiopia, I met my brother-in-law who was stationed as a army colonel at Ferfer border near Hiiran region then I told him that I was traveling to Dagabur, Ethiopia.

My brother was so sick then I personally decided to visit him so, he could give some accommodation and tell my traveling information to the rest of the family in Mogadishu City. I needed not to expose my travel.

It was okay to meet him!

After leaving Ferfer border checkpoint then we entered into Ethiopia. I've never been to Ethiopia for more than 34 years so, I didn't know what to do because I wanted to know exact how people were living?

I wanted to know if my family were no longer a target for Derge Military Regime! I really knew that it was the same as Somalia because once there is a martial law then they all use the same applications and tactics to suffocate civilians.

I was so scared to know more facts in Ethiopia! It'd been worse than even the Somali military regime, and many innocents were missing in action so, who to blame? I definitely knew that there wasn't democracy in Ethiopia too.

I won't be silent!

I recorded everything on the way to Dagabur while many people on the lorry asked me if I was working for a company.

"They asked for me," "If I was having a plan to spy on Ethiopia." I didn't surprise why they asked me for this question. I profoundly met their challenges on the lorry anyhow; some even thought that I was a high ranking officer.

"I couldn't explain it well," "Because this environment was so hostile to many innocent people," "A Majority of people still remembered how Somali and Ethiopia fought the war for the liberation of Somali Region in Ethiopia which colonialists handed over to Ethiopia."

I loved Somalis!

I hated the war as it'd inflicted painful memories to many people in the Horn of Africa, and it was very clearly that Somalia won the war against Ethiopia when Ethiopia was getting full support financially, technically and militarily from abroad.

As I knew that we beat Ethiopia well before, and I'm positively to beat them in the future if they try to abuse democracy in the Horn of Africa. It was also clear that Ethiopia hired foreign mercenary armies to fight alongside the weak Ethiopian forces during 1977 until 1988.

I told them that I was proud to be a Somalian!

They all laughed at me, and one of the passengers on the lorry was a double agent who came from Somalia, and he told me that he'd arrest me if I don't stop talking and sharing my idea openly in Ethiopia.

I don't hate the Ethiopian people! I only hate the Ethiopian Derge regime! So, if you're par of the Derge intelligence then I'd be in trouble so, I must listen to your advice however; you've been spying on innocent people.

I couldn't understand him well!

I kept quiet till we reached a town where we stopped to eat then he invited me to talk with him personally, and he told me that he knew my husband's name and what he does in Mogadishu City. He was on this lorry to visit his family in Dagabur.

He didn't like me to talk and share ideas on the lorry as everyone has a problem. And I didn't know who was my enemy or a friend. He told me that I was luck to talk because many persons on board knew him well that he was intelligence officer.

Did I care for him? I never wanted to meet him.

It was a coincide opportunity!

We talked more about life in Ethiopia, and he told me that he married a Somali lady from Dagabur town, and his was a Somali so that he could help me to find my brother if he was arrested and staying in a jail.

And my brother was only sick!

I told him that my brother was sick, and he never did a crime to go to jail in Ethiopia then he told me that it was easy to send someone to jail because everyone was afraid of the Derge military regime which had the worse justice in the world.

I was so terrified to listen his awkward and absurd tactics!

I stared not talking much because he told me that thousands are serving jail terms which didn't even deserve so, I realized that I could be like them too then I changed my shaped tone to another silly frequency.

“I didn't like the injustice practices in Ethiopia,” “It terrorized me to shut my mouth up,” “I couldn't tolerate it.” I've been escaping away from injustice practices from Somalia so, it's the same in Ethiopia. What's wrong with Africans?

I tactfully want to know the truth!

After we ate the lunch then we boarded on the lorry to move then someone came to the driver, and he told that there were a group of guerrilla fighters who've been trying to liberate Ogadenia, the Somali region in Ethiopia.

I knew it well when they said that there were a group of guerrilla fighters, it was the Ogaden National Libratation Front (ONLF). I was exciting internally because they were fighting for a real liberation for the people in the Somali regime which the mafia colonialists annexed to Ethiopia illegally.

I loved to meet the freedom fighters of the Ogaden National Libratation Front (ONLF).

I asked the intelligence officer, would you mind? If we go now, I really wanted to meet these guerrilla fighters so, I could say to them, please let's continue our struggle then he wasn't glad to know my wish for them.

Propitiously, I was ready to meet the true freedom fighters in the Somali regime willy-nilly.

I knew that anytime there should be a war between the Ethiopian Derge forces and the Ogaden Liberation Front however; I reached safely Dagabur town when I met my brother who was very sick, and he told me that he'd a complicated silliness.

I told my brother that I met someone on the lorry who was a double agent then he said to me; did you give him our address?

“I said to my brother,” “No, “I didn't give him our address.”

Okay! I'll be booking two tickets to fly back to Mogadishu City by tomorrow, we're not safe to stay in Dagabur town so, let's go to Addis Ababa tonight.

Then we'd driven to Addis Ababa where we booked two tickets then we'd flown to Mogadishu City within 24 hours so, he was so afraid of the Ethiopian Derge intelligence officer. We're luck to return to Mogadishu City.

# Chapter 13

Having had several problems in my family, I decided to go abroad with my family. Inexorably, the Somali Military Regime in-charge the country had been controlling the influx of travelers to abroad for many reasons including their security.

I ordered our passports at the Somali Immigration Directorate where after three days they called for questions why my children and I want to travel abroad? Certainly, we must prove that our travel to abroad was genuine.

I worried so badly!

The Somali Immigration Directorate issued my passport however; they rejected to issue my children's passports because they didn't want minors to leave the country so, they could indoctrinate their revolutionary supremacy.

Well, we're living in a nation where martial law was key to even solve civil court cases. And if you dare to say something rightly opposite to the interests of the Somali Military Regime then you're public enemy number one.

I wasn't interesting in their scary questions so, it's obvious that you could seek someone within the Somali Military Regime who'd a higher rank so, he might guarantee your safety passage. It was the only style to get everything done in the country.

I wasn't a bribing thief!

So many did crimes wrongfully in the country!

Some were even above the law because they're part the on-going organized crimes, and I didn't want to live in a crime invested country where democracy meant to kill opponents so that the world shouldn't know that was going on in the country's judicial system.

I've never screwed up before so, I wished to get my children's passport too.

I was so shaking when I entered the Somali Immigration Directorate Office in Mogadishu City, and I asked for the officer who sent me the letter. As I was waiting for the Officer then I met a lady who'd narrated me another shocking story.

She said to me; look! I was arresting for applying family passports more than 6 months, and they're still asking for me the same question at the Somali Immigration Directorate Office so, I want you to be strong woman if they apply it for you the same way.

I was personally feared about it!

I didn't like such bad story to listen!

I told her to be silent!

"She'd laughed at me," "She said clearly that I was as a target as the pullet to kill innocents." Adding that I wasn't innocent to apply for family passports to travel abroad which meant that I was opposing the work of the Somali Revolutionary Regime.

This shocked me further the way that she's been explaining to so, I thought that she was also an immigration officer who was trained to investigate and terrorize women in order to dig more secrets of their traveling needs to abroad.

I philologically asked her; how long have you been working at the Somali Immigration Directorate Office? I know that you're Officer Shamsa, and I was the embroidery teacher of your older sister Fahmo!

I know really who you are?

She laughed nicely!

She said to me; oh! You know me well!

Yes, I'm Officer Shamsa! You're welcome here, you're my teacher too but I want you to know that they ordered me to incriminate a case which I couldn't accept it. Anyhow; you'd get your children's passports soon.

If you get them by next week please, I advise you to leave soon because the Somali Military Regime had been planing to impose more restricted rules for applying passports because they noticed a number of people were escaping from the country.

And you're one these escaping people!

Okay! Officer Shamsa, my children and I will soon leave to neighboring Kenya so, we can rearrange our traveling options to Europe. I love Sweden or America because I want my children to grow up in democratic and more peaceful countries.

It's not been simple for us to apply for passports and not answer your shocking questions; I won narrowly to get what I need for my children properly, and I wish every parent will follow my trick in the near future.

I wasn't happy to live in my country under the Somali Military Regime!

And I couldn't get help to find my stolen kid so, would I need to stay in hostile environment? Positively, I want to live in exile so, I could only return to Somalia if and when the Somali Military Regime is no longer in power.

It was clear for me that the Somalia was heading into more chaotic and anarchic nation if the Somali Military Regime stayed in power for more than now so, this led me seek for external refuge before everything collapses in Somalia.

I meant to leave with my children!

I promised not expose my travel plans to my neighbors because they could shout and organize a crowd to expose my wishes. It's very common among Somalis to talk and share information without asking for it.

I left the Somali Immigration Directorate Office with all my passports, and I knew that there were some officers who'd be watching my movements before we leave Somalia so, I wanted to keep in low profile so, everyone should stay safe.

I don't want to cause neighborhood problems!

I informed to my husband that my children's passports were ready now, and we'd leave Somalia by the next week. Although he didn't accept our traveling plans before then he told me that it was now okay to leave the country.

Because many rebellious and tribally organized factions had been planned to overthrow this brutal and dictatorial military regime so, it's now safer if we leave early before they start a war which many innocent people may suffer from.

Truly, I knew that many rebellious and tribal organized factions were planing to fight with the Somali Military Regime in control.

Haven't I tried to leave before it happened? Then we'd have suffered from it costly!

Well, Somalia was now at war with its military regime in control. I called my cousin in German, Europe to rent an apartment and a car so, we arrive in Berlin, Germany then we'd normally catch up life in the country.

Ardently, I've no fear from the Somali Immigration Directorate Office because they've already cleared our traveling plan to abroad therefore; we didn't expect some other restrictions which could stop us leaving Somalia.

I felicitously exited our travel!

I called my sister, and I told her that we're leaving the country then she said to me clearly that she was gleefully to stay in Somalia until the Somali Military Regime was overthrown, and the rule returns to civilians.

She giggled me well then I told her that I respected her decision to stay but I asked her what should she request from me?

She chuckled to me again, and she finally asked me to stay in the country.

I then asked her why did she want me to stay? Then she told me that she wanted my accompany in the country.

*Dr.Badal Kariye*

I truly canceled my travel plans to Berlin, Germany in order to please my sister's wish to accompany her in Somalia.

I love my sister Shukgri!

# Chapter 14

Having being planned to travel Berlin, German was canceled in order to please my sister's wish however; I knew that many people may ask for me traveling cancellation to abroad which my children and I were approved to leave Somalia.

I was exited to live in abroad!

After five days I received a police report which wasn't based on fact but rumors to incriminate innocent people as criminals so, they'd let the really thugs free people to enjoy more crimes and continue terrorize everyone.

I read this police report carefully, and I asked myself if there'd ever be justice for all under the Somali Military Regime because many people who've been working for the corrupted and the illegally stationed government in Somalia knew their crimes, and they'd not stop these crooked public servants.

I remembered many of the crimes in Somalia!

As I wanted to tell my children that we're not traveling to abroad then I asked my relatives if I could send some of my children to abroad so, they'd help us in the near future then every one of my close relatives rejected me to send the children to abroad.

Negatively, I didn't accept the advice of my close relatives therefore; I seek other consultations with ex-friends and school mates so, we could come up with effective and working decision to survive in the near future.

Well, every crime is the criminal's insanity!

I disliked to witness many innocent people pay hard prices to stay alive and work in the country if they bribe the crooked authorities which overthrew our civilian government. I want to survive and bring up my children wisely.

Had it been a democratic rule in the country? Everyone would like to stay, work and live in Somalia because there isn't place on this earth which can compete the calamity and the plentiful resources which bestowed to the people of Somalia.

I love my country and continent!

Sensibly, everyone loves Somalia! And the only reason which the colonial powers separated Somalis into five zones was a key to steal our plentiful resources in the future. If you don't understand what I mean then you'll understand it in the future.

I wasn't educated well however; I listened to many historical facts! If you want to leave our history and stop crimes in the country then you'd truly go and see how the colonialists are re-inventing their slavery tactics to control us one way or the other.

We don't need their foreign aid!

sagely, foreign aid to Somalia or other nations which some colonialists captured or ruled illegally was, is and will only be to enslave us indirectly so they can access and steal natural resource as it's now happening in many places around the world.

I really don't call it smart geopolitics! It's a greedy and cannibalistic geopolitics which favors few blood suckers while millions of innocent people are dying lack of medicine, access to purified water and food as well as environmental crisis.

Loot out the fact!

I'm not too old to tell history! I loved my country – Somalia! Anyhow; things in Somalia are getting worse. I can't solve everything, and I say something correctly to encourage others so, we can fix our falling nation.

Then I'd only be target to blame!

Who wants to confront? No one dared to say something about the dictatorial regime criminally. “They thought that everyone was interesting in their vision to rob and rule the people.” Well, it's now a part of the New Somali Culture!

Discerningly, I was told to keep quiet so, I'd not encourage others to see and analyze facts on the ground while they're constantly suffering from many crimes which the crooked public servants had been imposing since 1969 until then.

Don't waste time to correct a brutal regime!

I called angrily called the Hodan Police Station where I asked them if they'd receive any information leading to find my stolen child then the Police Officer on duty asked me who I was? And who gave me the station's commander phone number?

I said politely; can I talk to the crime investigator's desk?

“He laughed at me,” “And he asked me,” Why are you calling crime investigator's desk? Is someone missing? Or did someone steal something? Or are you looking for someone to take care business? Tell me now!

Or I'd hang up!

I foolishly answered one question! I told him that I was asking for some information about my stolen child at Banadir Hospital then he crisply hung up the phone while he was talking to another officer in the room.

I irritably cried to know that they're not investigating crimes as they occurred in the country, and every one was as corrupted as the devil. I've never understood that I was still a civilian who's not voice to speak or someone to speak for.

I seek a powerful voice to represent me!

I didn't understand why everyone wanted to lie publicly? Was it that bribery make cases to be solved quickly? What's going on? I want to get some justice, please can anyone help me to find my stolen newborn?

I'll pay you good!

The Police Officer rang my house's phone then I picked it up to talk then he asked me if my husband was working with the government then I laughed at him saying that he was really joking to call me to answer silly questions.

I told him that my husband has been a public servant and businessman for longtime, and he does his job with piety. We don't need corruption! So, he shouldn't call me ever on the phone unless they get some vital information about my stolen child.

Predominantly, we must be very clever!

I didn't know who was the caller from the Hodan Police Station? I'd not take risky call!

Well, everyone knows that the Somali Military Regime acted supremely in the country so, it credits every good job then I can't oppose everything at the same. I sometimes do guess work to avoid their brutal punishment.

My husband came, and he asked me if I got some information then I told him that he could go to the Hodan Police State where he might get some information then he said to me; I'm tired to go there now, I want to get some rest!

I'll go there later!

I know that he was trivially to go there!

I sat down to create a prose for all stolen babies and mothers. I couldn't talk the whole day with my children because they didn't know that I was creating a prose personally then everyone comes and goes without a say.

As I was brushing problems, I wanted some help!

I wont' surrender to criminal who'd been misleading people wrongfully, and I couldn't give bribes whether they like me or not. I loved my children so, I couldn't go to jail for no reason then I inveigled my life to act neutrality.

I've never impelled some people into trouble so, why would some people to allure us into trouble? Well, we say it, it's human nature! I don't doubt it but we must all get fair justice in this world so that everyone enjoys.

*Dr. Badal Kariye*

I love you all so, please you better seek and find my stolen child!

I'll pay you well!

# Chapter 15

as we say in this proverb; action speaks louder than words. I've spoken many times to encourage people so, we can fight against injustice and bribery corruption in the country, staunchly I accepted that people wanted to witness more criminal activities.

I wasn't interesting in bribery country where children were ready to be part of this inheriting corruptions so, I needed some help to leave country so, my children could get better education and enjoy good lifestyle.

I loved my country!

I contacted to the British and American embassies in Mogadishu so, they could offer me free investigators to search and look into my case. Then I was called that I've been employed as a spy master with foreign entities.

According to my understanding, I was betrayed by some Somali staff working at these foreign embassy who'd been working with the Somali National Security Services because they deemed to be the best, and they couldn't accept my request to third parties.

Well, I wasn't a member of group 4!

Trouble begins till it gets solution!

I was called at the Somali National Security Headquarters in Mogadishu, and they asked me if I'd received any donations from these two above-mentioned foreign embassies before I contacted them then I said no!

I seek extra intelligence help from these foreign embassies to search and locate my stolen kid, and this isn't a big problem to do so. I wanted their help to see how I wasn't getting exact what I wanted my government to do.

That was only it!

I was reliably decisive to seek extra offers!

Losing freedom in a country where martial law was the supreme law of the land would have been tough but I must comply with their request so, if they knew the facts then I thought that I'd be free. I never imagined that I was always be a target.

They're only targeting me for just one request which I made personally, and they're ready to punish my close relatives and even some neighbors. I didn't want the Military Regime to punish my close relative and neighbors.

And as I canceled to travel to abroad, it's weird to live in my country.

I can't tell everything in actuality!

Everyone made easy for my family to get away from this bribery and hostility invested country where if you say something correctly then it could simply turn it into wrong way. We wanted justice for all, and we didn't see it.

Saying right or wrong to the Somali Military Regime was a terrible decision anyhow; we mastered to manipulate them. I wasn't afraid of them as I've had the grounds to defend myself in the lunatic martial court.

No one love martial law!

Had they being able to know me before? No, so, who was working at the foreign embassies in Mogadishu City? Who told them my name? Which district I live in? And what was the reason for asking me many questions?

“I was really the victim of many counter secret agents.”

I didn't back up to tell the facts even if it was better than hell! I said it clearly to them so, they'd either arrest me or set up a phony sentence for life imprisonment, and they could possibly arrange for the death penalty.

African dictatorial regimes which are led by military leaders are same in many aspects but the worse should be the one who habituates to arrest or kill his own people, and it was happening in Somalia where no one dared to confront them.

I saw many crimes in the country!

Those Sheiks who'd legally confronted their injustice, well, the Somali Military Regime sent them to the hereafter life so, no one should dare to challenge them in the rule of law and how they'd govern in Somalia.

Well, after killing the Sheiks illegally while they still thought that communism would prevail in the country so, the Western interests should also be limited then this was also dragging us out into more chaotic and anarchic retaliations among the Somali clans who tested the power itself before the military coup took place in Somalia.

We're all politicians!

Whatever you witnessed illegally! It was part of our responsibility because we've the right to stop it before it hurt or kill many innocent people. As we're not above the law, who made the Somali Military Regime to act above the constitution?

I think that if people unified to stand up and defend freedom then nothing would have dared to stop them but some of us were working with the Somali Military Regime for many reasons, and this practice applies for reporting rebellious acts in the country.

We stop crimes now!

Legitimately, I was also a champion of justice but the Somali Military Regime captured the country then I kept myself in low profile because I didn't want to invite problems. I could only go to my embroidery shop.

But stealing my newborn boy made me to learn a lot in the country, and the Somali Security Forces are corrupted. I've no money to bribe them so, I was confused, and I've no got kind offers in my country. What hell was going on?

Well, I called it dump world! As they said: charity begins home!

Are we ready to clean up corruptions? Or are we ready to legalize it? I was never too old to learn! I've mastered to ask for questions but they often answered me badly then I considered everything except bribery or corruption.

I hate all the illegal activities in the country.

I can't answer your question, I'm not spy-master so, I'm a Somalia who's been requesting for external assistance. I didn't know why they wanted to border me? However; I answered whatever they wanted to know so, they must stop sending letters to my home.

I want walking freely in Mogadishu City!

I've denounced my nationality so, I didn't understand what they wanted me to suffer from. I've never joined with foreign club in the country nor did I ever ask for money to help my family? So, I was only the victim of the counter spy masters.

I've not even heard information about my stolen kid. Whoever kidnapped him from his cradle at the Banadir Hospital? I wasn't easy prey as I learned to communicate with foreign embassies and organizations for further assistance.

I didn't accept our government's scare tactics!

It didn't make sense to all! We'd not only watch crimes but we're sometimes part of the game! If you see something wrong them we're obliged to reject it willy-nilly however; our fear let such crimes strive and damage us undoubtedly.

As we've not been stopping criminal acts in the country, it affected everyone indirectly or directly while those who're working with the Somali Military Regime are the most extreme corrupted people in the Horn of Africa.

My antipathy to this criminal act isn't working well! We love our country to prosper socially and economically however; we knew that the Somali Military Regime would improve lives for awhile but they'd turn more brutal if we didn't obey them.

I don't want to say something unlawfully.

# Chapter 16

Africa is birth place of mankind so, it's also possible to be the birth place of everything else well, I didn't doubt it. I know that many people may think silly to ask questions when you're paranoiac mood in this world.

My was stolen in a daylight!

I wished to know who the real thug was? However; it seemed to me that it'd had been planned for some reason. I'm innocent mother, and I didn't really do bad thing in the country. Why did they target my child?

As we've not won the hearts of our parents in the past then could it be possible? We're all cursed to suffer from our parental disobedience. "I'm not clean," "Maybe," "We must remember it well." My family and I did nothing wrong.

We don't need a punishment!

Equality is very important to every society, and we're getting equal services in this legal system so, are we able to hire external lawyers? And if we do hire external lawyers then we're sure that we'll face more punishable codes in this country.

We've never requested to hire people externally! It's not wise thing to do, and I can't risk my family. I can't live in a constant fear because I'm human being. One day I must surrender to confront my ideas in this world.

Let's take care each other!

Africa is a place where you may see many things, I'm really confused! If you're not the boss or master then you must become a chief or a master to take care everything. As we're not aware whatever is going on in Africa? I love to see it in the near future.

I can't sing well in Somalia!

"We're all victimized prisoners," "We're not welcome to know more facts in the country." I didn't understand them, All I understood, it was how to pay a bribery so, the corrupted public servants may enjoy to buy anything.

Surely, many public servants chew Khat literally meaning Catha edulis! This Catha edulis loses their money and time, and most of them chew after lunch as if it was prescribed by satanic doctors while the growers of the Catha edulis makes billions.

I saw how this terrible Catha edulis causes many medical and family problems!

We must stop it now!

Catha edulis is a drug!

I couldn't forget to tell you the truth, and this is what force a majority of the public servants in the Horn of Africa to ask for bribes and break the law so, they can buy, sit and enjoy with their Catha edulis in cafeterias, shops or homes.

This is a big matter!

So, how can a corrupted government officials seeking Catha edulis help innocents like? We talk truly, and we must tell them to stop such crimes before this country is out of control. We're all guilty if we watch their illegal activities in the country.

Once illegal then it's possible to mislead people!

I love my stolen newborn but for the time I've been searching to rescue him then I learned a lot in this martial system, and the only way it'd collapse, they must use drugs like Catha edulis, wind or other harmful things.

Well, you can only talk if you've superior leaders within the government so, they can let you go free if and when the martial authority arrests you in the country. Should I avoid to hide my feeling against the on-going crimes? I never wanted to shut up!

I can't shut up!

As I knew that innocent civilians weren't able to discuss everything openly, and had they able to expose? No one dared to say that he or she's enough to tolerate criminals in the country, and the bribery practicing had also been affecting the whole security forces.

Where was the responsibility? Drugs after lunch!

We couldn't deny the fact!

By the way, I could give money to my case investigators! I wasn't that rich to pay something, and if they asked me to offer extra fees to please them the I'd be worrying the entire day or night until I get something right.

Will they be nice to help? Ask for information! Well, we're living in a country where martial con men wanted to deny and suffocate democracy as well as culture and religion but they only allowed us to accept and behave to adapt communism.

Why are we all actors for crimes against humanity?

We're Muslims! The country was an Islamic nation, so, why did the Somali Military Regime impose communism? And why did the West to dismantle Somali Military Regime? It was a gambling game for the Somalia untapped natural resources.

I can't deny the facts now! We're not helping the innocents in the country!

Some foreign nations wanted us to dismantle Somalia!

Who wasn't able to welcome the Somali Military Regime? Everyone welcomed them to take up leadership, and people thought that they could root out tribalism and nepotism but they're part of the problematic extension of refueling tribalism and nepotism among clans.

Generally, speaking the truth about bribery and corruptions, it'd easily stop more bribes or corrupted officials to rethink and comply with the law before they're caught in a red handed crimes which the blue laws would have to conscript them.

We must all love the country!

We're not above the constitution!

I knew that those criminal investigators on my case were both once mobsters so, I didn't understand how the Somali Military Regime hired ex- gang members as security agents in this country, and if you say that you know them then you're trouble.

I'm not a troublemaker!

I only love the truth!

If we can't stop crimes then we're all rioters for injustice county. Have I been mad? Perhaps, when you're innocent, if you became a victim, and the Police must help you to stop crimes but if they're part of the organized crime then what should I do? I must use wisdom!

I wished that they can read the Holy Qur'aan instead of wasting money and time for drugs. As time is good to benefit it, and if possible to help the needy for anything including offers which you can offer kindly without show off.

We're not dead!

Wake up people!

I called the Somali Police Headquarters in Mogadishu City for any leading information then I was asked for a question which I couldn't answer it right way. Did I know the answer? I was never asked such question before!

You ask me your questions!

"I'm a Somalian mother who's been seeking her stolen child at Banadir Hospital," "And I didn't understand such question." Am I the thug? Why I called the Somali Police Headquarters? I only wanted to know any further information about my stolen child.

If you don't have information then I'll call you another day. Bye!

*Dr. Badal Kariye*

No, don't  hang up! The Police will call you soon!

I hung up the phone furiously without saying goodbye!

# Chapter 17

As I was physically, emotionally and psychologically tired to walk with, ask for and answer many questions then I went to visit Villa Somalia which was literally meaning the Office of the Presidency for extra help.

I wasn't able to enter at the visiting pavilion because I didn't look like a rich or a government official so, this made a challenge for me to get access. Definitely, I wasn't paying bribes or phony smile to act that I was happy with the Somali marshal law.

And I didn't contemplate well!

Had we been exonerated? "This was a question that I'd not able to answer." Everyone was thinking that if he or she was working with government then they'd obligation to ask for bribes or suffocate people like me.

Anyhow: I was a market guru who learned many trickery styles of the Somali Security Forces, and I'd apply for my skill if and when they corners me. It didn't seem that I knew many of their trickery skill so, I'd stop them.

They can't tantalize a market guru!

I waited for more 3 hours to enter this Villa Somalia!

I knew that my presence would agitate many people at Villa Somalia because I was wearing old fashion cloth which most of the people at the presidential pavilion didn't like to see but everyone has had a reason to come and ask for a solution.

I was there to apply for extra help! I wanted to share important information with the president so, he could solve crimes and enforce his marshal law to stop bribes and other corrupted cases in the country. That was the only reason I visited his office.

That was it!

After I came back from Villa Somalia then everyone at Sigalle Market suspected that I was a spy agent then I was so confused to explain. During this period then everyone was also suspicious to know how many people were working secretly with the Somali Military Government.

I was afraid of my life!

It's easy to set up someone in Africa than other continent because we don't comply with the law. As matter of fact I was seeking for help to find my stolen newborn however; they thought that I was an undercover agent.

I wasn't undercover agent!

I've never applied for an undercover job with the government.

*Dr. Badal Kariye*

I've notified my family I was viewed whenever I tell someone that I even went to the Villa Somalia for help where I was even denied access to enter several hours before they let me sit at the pavilion. I never met someone to help me.

I was truly helpless!

I loved my people but the country is in total trouble so, can I accept to become part of this problem? No! I don't to want disrupting people in the Sigalle Market so, I decided to move out to new location in Bakaraha Market.

Someone encouraged me to relocate to Hamarweyne Market where there were many different businesses. I told him that I was moving out to Bakaraha Market where I love buy milk for my children.

That is good for me!

I really thanked you for that!

We've been victims of the Somali Military Regime, and everyone fears for his or her life in the country because they can come after you, and they charge you for nothing so, you'll stay the rest of your life in behind bar.

I want to rest now!

Once upon time I heard there was a King in the Horn of Africa, and his name was called Diiftire who was very powerful as many historians explained his reign. As we're Somalis, we must know our history well.

We're only corrupted but we've had history for transparency and accountability in the horn of Africa under the kingdom of Diiftire King so, we can still apply for his rules thereby; everyone can live in Somalia and in this world peacefully.

But we can accept to live under this marshal law!

I don't know if people should care transparency, accountability and trustworthy in Somalia! People are turning into more corrupted deals which we can't even solve or settle it in the legal system as everyone hates the marshal law.

I didn't want to blame people unless I witnessed what people were talking about when they meet officials within the government. I knew that corruption is a key to any problematic issue in the country. I've never witnessed it before.

I've not missed my time!

We must educate people to know that we care about our life!

I hate to lie!

Accepting the wrong blame wasn't easy task for me so, I attempted hardly to seek extraordinary assistance. After years in power he's not been a good leader whom the people loved so much, and I was wrong to visit his office for help.

I'd say nothing against his regime until they find my stolen newborn baby.

It's wise to ask for help!

"I didn't image that I'd be another victim," "A majority of the people had never questioned the legitimacy of the Somali Military Regime," "We're still afraid of saying something against them. And they can't find my stolen newborn.

I was a good drawer for many things!

I called my mother to come Mogadishu City so, I could leave the children with her. After I made my first call then I was called from the Somali National Security Services Headquarters for questioning because they wanted to know what are my connections in Ethiopia.

I only had family who'd been living in the Ogaden Region which was given illegally to the Ethiopian Emperors, and as we know that even Somalia began war to liberate the Somali region of Ogadenia militarily.

Where is my newborn baby?

Who stole him?

Why am I not getting help?

They stupidly answered to me, lady, we called you to answer our questions. We're not here to answer your questions so, if you don't want to answer us then we'd arrest you. Do you know Godka? Godka is literally the Hole Jail!

I heard it many times before, and I didn't want them to arrest me, I was so frightened. I shake badly, and I said to them that I was ready to answer their questions. I've not been ready to misinform any information which I got during my search.

No jokes!

Wastefully, they laughed at me then they said to me that I wasn't telling the truth. I'd not option to decide what to do next at their intelligence headquarters. I was thinking to jump through the window if they decided to arrest me.

I didn't like if they wanted to detain me for no reasons!

*Dr. Badal Kariye*

I said to them that I wanted to hire a lawyer so, they can talk to him in the court.

And I stood up saying goodbye!

# Chapter 18

As I was worried about the bribery and corruptions, I didn't understand how it was hard to mislead innocent people? If there is no justice then who is responsible? Everyone was sick to listen their bogus propaganda through public media.

I contemplated the injustice for many reasons.

We've not seen a country where the police, justice & officials are all corrupted to ask for bribes so they can give you misleading information, and they'd incriminate you any crimes as it occurred many time before.

It's very clear that we've seen enough!

I sat down in a special public garden at the Bakaraha intersection. I asked my life if I'd ever meet my stolen newborn boy. It was a challenging visionary mission to think my little world so, I could get solutions.

I love my children!

I've not done it well!

My resourceful responsibility is to search and coordinate with the search and rescue efforts for my stolen child. I generated many questions and answers with the beautifully growing graze in this Bakaraha intersection.

I've no equivalent brainstorm to march against this injustice corruption!

I tried to recognize their mission!

I couldn't invite other problems, and I called my husband by dreaming emotionally in this beautiful garden. Had they been known me where I was sitting some rest? Peacefully, I didn't want to invite their problems.

I remembered many things which I used to rethink my strategic plan for search and rescue the stolen newborn. It's human error to make mistakes, and we must get solutions for better understanding what are root cause of these endless corruptions in the country.

I don't like to pay bribes!

As I've not witnessed my mistakes before then I realized it after I delivered my baby. Everyone was asked for information, and no one came forward to answer one single question to the crime investigators.

“I was thinking that no one could solve my case.”

I say where is my stolen child?

Who can tell me where to find him? I'll pay money because I'm loving him every second so, can anyone relief my stress? I know that his father hasn't tried the best to search him because he's a public servant.

I heard the calling prayer's call!

I walked out of the Bakaraha intersection where I've been resting for 4 hours to think about my need to find the stolen child. Many people surprised me that I was crazy to enter the garden without someone else accompanying.

I didn't care because I was taking some rest. I didn't like people to come with and border however; I enjoyed the sounds of birds and walking of small animals in the garden. It's not been easy for people to know that I was having family problems.

I didn't shout well!

I walked out of the public garden!

I never astonished!

I know that my people are innocent, and I know that these corrupted public servants won't report ther crimes to their superiors, maybe, their superiors are corrupted too. So, how I can correct such corrupted officials?

I didn't waste my time to figure out!

After having no satisfied such bribery requests and continuous corruptions in my country then I've decided to travel in abroad so, I could relax for some time. I knew that my children shouldn't accept my travel only.

Have I not been fair to tell the truth? Well, there are always some mistakes, and I can do it too. Some people didn't like to comment their mistakes. I couldn't blame them so, I'd have done it in the same ways.

I wasn't ready to sign wrong papers!

I call the Somali Police Headquarters in Mogadishu City so, I can ask them if they've information for my case. A policewoman answered my call after it rung, and she asked me who I was? Why I called the Somali Police Headquarters?

I told her that I was a victim, and my case number was number # 23123454! I wanted to know if the Police got some important information. "She said to m," "Your case number # 23123454 has been closed down for 2 days ago.

Who closed my case number # 23123454!?

I didn't know it!

Please you can tell me exactly who has closed down my number # 23123454? I must know it now. I've been waiting for help. This is another shocking answer to listen and know it now. Please I'm a mother, so, you can guess how I'm deeply worried for the stolen child? You help me now!

I want no proves!

What I should expect from the Somali Police? They've given bad information, and they explained to me how they closed down my number # 23123454? Is this an acceptable answer to worrying mother? I deeply resented it.

I can't jump over it!

"The Policewoman asked if I was still married." Where is your husband? We want to talk and ask for questions. Pleas you can go and find him then if you find him, you can call me this direct telephone number # 999999.

Goodbye now.

I cried sadly!

Am I crazy? Or was it possible to listen her bad report? Whoever closed down my number # 23123454? He's responsible for many crimes which he intentionally closed down for take extra bribes. And I don't know If I'll ever get justice in this country.

I run to my embroidery shop at Bakaraha Market! I told the bad report to my business neighborhood and every client who came in my shop. I said clearly that there is no justice so, if they go to any police station then they must take some pocket money.

Well, I know the Mafia!

I don't ask for help withing the Somali Military Regime, I've seen enough to know the truth. They're not ready to help the Somali people. It's true that they don't want to solve cases as first come first serve but if you pay bribes then you'll seen quick solutions.

Can anyone get my information about my stolen child? I'll pay enough money!

We can't shape th future if they'd always ask for bribes.

Surely, I can't accept this corruption!

I invested many experts for my case, and many of them knew that if they investigated it then they'd be in trouble. Somalia was heading into the wrong direction where we won't stop it. Let's tell the truth and stop crimes.

*Dr. Badal Kariye*

I love my country!

Let's stop their crimes!

# Chapter 19

I called a medical doctor who's been stationed in Nairobi, Kenya to come and treat me for stress because there was very terrible pain which I was suffering from. I couldn't trust Somali doctors to cure in regard to corruptions.

Even though medical treatment was free in the country but I didn't trust it. I thought that I made many mistakes for accusing and making more complaints against governmental bribery and corruption so, I could be public enemy number!

They don't know where is my stolen child? Nor do I know it!

Specifically, we're all afraid of this martial law!

As we know many educated and intellectuals have been fleeing from Somalia because they didn't want to accept the martial law as the law of the land, and It seemed to me that I couldn't womanize for it then I'd always be in trouble!

So, would I be as busy? I'll have be busy to work with the criminal investigators until they get some important information that may lead us to the conclusion of my case's fact while the real thug or thugs are behind black hole.

Yes, we know the jail!

Some mafia won't like penitentiary!

Who are cool the blooded killers? The thug or thugs! Or the martial law which describes that there is no other law to work in a nation whenever it's based on illegally by a group rebellious military bandits who're also fed up with civil indoctrination of democracy.

Well, there is always a smoke to hide their crimes in a nation where majority of people were illiterate and stilling catching up the rest of the world. Thought, the martial law provide free education and health coverage which many sovereign nations were still trying to provide to their citizens.

Somalia was still one step ahead of many nations in Africa and many other parts in the world.

No surprises in Somalia! As we told many big nations that we don't like colonialists. They didn't understand what our leaders have been telling and teaching them for centuries, and they thought that we could easily swallow their indoctrination.

However; after they cut foreign aid to the Somali Military Regime then all Somali public servants were working without salary for months then what happened was to ask for briber for public services including for applying internal and external scholarships.

I didn't astonish it!

"So many countries misunderstood us."

*Dr. Badal Kariye*

Did anyone call me for update? Never! I called the Somali Police Headquarters in Mogadishu, no one was answering the telephone because the time I called the Somali Police Headquarters was a lunch time.

Many of the security officers were either eating their lunch or they went to buy Khad for westing time and money. Amazingly, they didn't get sufficient salary but they used to get more bribes to cover its costs.

I don't like shits!

I love my children, and I know that their country is now heading into more corruptions where transparency, accountability and trustworthy is a crime to civilians if and whenever they talk about it So, are we all fools? No!

We love Africa! We must stop internal and external corruptions.

We're not sure to know more about internal or external corruptions however; I came to know it only while I was searching my stolen child where everyone whom I met that was working with the Somali Military Regime were asking for bribes.

A lot of shits with this corrupted military revolution!

I can't sleep unless I and my family get back our stolen newborn. I've been working with many sectors within the Somali Military Regime so, they could spread my word to the general public at all levels where they can help me and others in the future.

We're afraid of this corrupted martial law! It's not above the international law so, I believed that it'd leave us one day in the near future notwithstanding; we mustn't destroy the country with bribes and inviting external corruptions.

I knew too many corrupted contracts were illegally given to private foreign entities!

Haven't we seen foreign investors to land grabbing agricultural lands? Who let them to grab agricultural lands? It's the military regime, so can you deny it? I knew the fact which many of the pubic servants should disagree with me.

"We're not accepting their invention of artificial intelligence."

We're must get better solutions to such bribery and corrupted cases in the country otherwise; people may get angry and start more rebellious activities in order to overthrow the Somali Military Regime which call itself nowadays the Democratic Republic of Somalia.

Where is democracy? They screwed up and discarded the democratically approved constitution when the Somali Military Regime took up power in bloodless coup d'etat On 21st October, 1969 until now on. We can't talk

No laughing, it's true!

So, don't crazy in Somalia!

As we tell that there are many crimes related in bribes and corrupted contracts which most of the high ranking public servants used to apply for their favors then I knew that the innocent people like me needed a loud voice to expose it.

Surely, I wanted justice!

I'm fed with bribes and corruptions! I've working on odd jobs, and I some worked at my embroidery shop where even Mogadishu Municipal Officers come for asking taxes everyday so, how I feel it? Everything is painful nowadays!

Lightly, it's not easy!

We love Somalia, and we stop criminals regardless of who they work for? If justice is not served equally to all then we're on the wrong path to destroy our country, and before we all fall in this unknown crisis then we must work for a good governance.

The past two weeks I was contemplating how I'd expose bribery? I knew that all newspapers and journals were produced by the government itself thus, it'd the total control for sharing and propagating news and other important information in the country and around the world.

Everything was under the full control of the regime in-charge!

So, I couldn't get access to publish one article for showing how to correct the corrupted officials? Then I invited many people to com and meet me at the embroidery shop at Baraha Market in Mogadishu City where we discussed issues of bribes and corruptions.

I knew that some of the women who came to my discussion were married to military colonels and generals in the government so, they can spread my word to the public before the remaining doctors and intellectuals flee from the country.

I'd advise to expose the truth!

Well, it's the best time for our people to know who're the criminals? We don't want to flee from our country so, we've all the responsibility to correct our mistakes collectively therefore; our enemy must always lose in Somalia.

Is it fair game? Yes, we can do it.

We're all off-spring of Aden and Eve! So, why are we fighting for? Well, is it to survive? I don't know how I'll survive the rest of my life if I won't get back my stolen newborn. And I won't move out from Mogadishu City till something big forces me to flee from it.

*Dr. Badal Kariye*

I better say to all look before you leap!

Let's leak the crimes!

## Chapter 20

I've flown to Addis Ababa, Ethiopia to visit my sister who's been living there for many years, and I wanted to share my vision about family and Somalia. I've 1 month visa to stay in Ethiopia where I heard more information about multiracial communities live in side by side.

After my second day in Addis Ababa then I woke up early in the morning so I can visit and buy something from Addis Ababa markets. I didn't want to hire a translator because I learned Amharic when I was young sheepherder.

My sister's little son accompanied to walk out then we rented a taxi. Had we no money? Then it's very difficult to visit markets in Addis Ababa.

As we're going through the old traffic lights then we've seen ex- Ethiopian generals who've been beggars, and they begged us to give them something. Unfortunately, some of these beggars spoke Somali language because they learned it from the Somali Ogadenia Region where they either grew up or they worked in as officers for long time.

No surprises in Addis Ababa!

Then we gave them out some Ethiopia Birrs, and we asked them if they participated the Somalian-Ethiopian wars then one of them laughed at me, and he said to me that he'd not fight for Ethiopia because people are fed up with the current corrupted tribal regime. He wished the western world to either assassinate or poison the Mafia leader in-Charge.

We don't get our retirement benefits! We're Ethiopian veterans who're now beggars!

I remembered that I saw the same Somali veteran people who also became beggars in Somalia while those who've never fought for the country had been enjoying everything in the country. So, who's not veteran? I was also another guru to detect that there is organized crimes which government imposed on innocent people.

As I knew that Ethiopia literally as Abyssinia was also always a place where people came for refugee then they used to get it but Ethiopia is nowadays a place where animosity and refueling conflicts starts in many ways therefore; I didn't think that I could get help in Addis Ababa.

I asked for the taxi driver to stop at the Ethiopian National Museum.

I wanted to read if Ethiopia has collected many multicultural art facts from African nations and the world at large, and when we entered to the first door of the Ethiopian National Museum then I saw a mother who was carrying a child and he was directing her husband to graze their animals.

Then I totally remembered how I lost my newborn baby after I delivered him at Banadir Hospital.

A very kind lady came to us, and she asked me why did I stop at this photo? Then I told her my reason. She shouted loudly then we're not sure why she shouted? I then ran after her to stop and ask what was the problem? Well, she said to me that she'd lost a child too.

And whenever she visits this Ethiopian National Museum, and she sees this photo which remembers her lost child!

I hugged her well!

"I told her that she'd get her lost child in one a day which no one can hide anything."

As I was explaining my sympathy then she asked me if I could give her a job to do in Addis Ababa because she was struggling to buy the university fees of her two sons at the Addis Ababa University.

I told her that I wasn't visiting Addis Ababa for a vocation but I came here to discuss with my sister so, she could give an advice about our family business.

Allowing her that I wasn't capable to offer some job then she smiled. She said to me that she understood my problem well, and we'd the same issue then she suggested to me if we could ask for our governments to stop wars so, other mothers in the near future won't encounter the same problems.

"Well," "We could see that mothers in these two warring neighbors didn't like a war."

I hugged her once again then I gave her out 100 Birr!

I asked the cap driver that if we can go to the biggest market in Addis Ababa.

We went to Merkato which is one of the biggest open markets in Africa where we wanted to visit and buy some stuff. As we're entering the Merkato then many people asked us what we want to buy? I didn't only want to buy something but I want to know what items they've in Merkato?

We must see it!

I walked only inside the Merkato! I was dressing my Somali cultural cloth. Ethiopia is one of the most diversified countries in the world, and It didn't border anyone except few thugs who wanted to snatch my purse. I knew their faces as they followed us up inside the Merkato.

I bought some fruits!

Then we headed back to our home at Pole area in Addis Ababa.

My sister asked for me if I saw something different than Mogadishu Markets. Then I mentioned that I've never ever seen open market like the Merkato Market. I told her that I bought some fruits and stuff then she laughed at me, and she said it that it was good to accompany me but She wasn't interesting in.

I asked her how many times per week she goes to shop at Merkato? Then she told me once a week.

I said that it was good to go and visit Merkato Market where I bought some fruits and shop.

I asked my sister if she learned Amharic then she said to me that she speaks broken Amharic. I didn't understand why she didn't like to learn Amharic.

Well, she didn't go to school all her life. As I wanted to welcome her back to Somalia so, I encouraged her to go to adult school so that sh may learn something.

My sister told me that she'd not come back to Somalia because she didn't like the same military regime in-charge the county, and she left Somalia after she encountered instability where some government officials threatened her to kill if she exposed what they're doing in Mogadishu City.

She didn't like their crimes!

I've been analyzing many issues in Addis Ababa, and I saw same crimes in Mogadishu are going on in Addis Ababa. I don't want to stay in Ethiopia so, I'll fly to Nairobi, Kenya soon.

My sister invited me to travel with her family to hyena herder who feeds and talks with hyenas however; I was so scared to accompany with her to visit the hyena herder.

I didn't know it how to explain but I told my sister that I was planning to go to Nairobi.

She accepted my travel to Nairobi, and she told me that she'd soon visit me when I go back to Mogadishu. I excited her announcement then I called my family in Mogadishu to let them know that my sister will visit us soon so, they must prepare her a vacant room.

Then I bagged my stuff, and I booked a flight ticket to Nairobi.

I farewell my sister, relatives and friends whom I met in Addis Ababa.

I've flown to Nairobi at 4:00 PM so, I could get some relatives to pick me up at the Jomo Kenyatta International Airport.

I met on board a Somali Kenyan businesswoman who's also some businesses in Somalia and Ethiopia, and we'd a good discussion about lifestyle and profitable businesses in Africa then she told me that she was seeking a business partner in Somalia.

I told her that Somalis are now growing entrepreneurs in the Horn of Africa so, it's possible to open few shopping malls in Nairobi. She was excited my idea, and she gave me her businesses card so, we'd be in touch.

Well, I knew that many Somalis live in Kenya and Ethiopia because the imperialists made a big mistake to divide Somalis but God's will helped Somalis to adapt and fight for their rights in the Horn of Africa.

Certainly, We're prospering in the Horn of Africa!

We slept for while until we arrived at the Jomo Kenyatta International Airport.

*Dr. Badal Kariye*

She was picked up then I rode a taxi to downtown Nairobi where I rented a lodge at Eastliegh Estate.

I slept until morning at 8:00 AM.

# Chapter 21

Coming to the Capital City of Nairobi wasn't a crazy idea but I knew that there are many professional doctors who may help me get out of personal stress. As I'd no money to cover my sojourn then I went to meet one of my relatives who's been living in Nairobi for than 30 years.

Fortunately, I got a ride to his business area at Eastleigh Estate where he wasn't present when I reached there.

I asked myself if I could immigrate my family to Nairobi, Kenya. Then it wasn't easy for me to do so.

I met some street children who're locally known as Chokora, and they're very happy to tell me many stories about life in Kenya. As one of them discussed with me the real challenges which they face daily where their civil dictatorial government hasn't been helping them for education and health coverage.

He said to me; we're called Chokara in our country!

We're worse than many but we're only poor, and most of the people in Kenya had been ignoring us that as if we're not here, lady, we're here to tell our history.

Well, every city has some kind of poor people but they've different issues in struggling life which some may get relief while others mayn't get it.

I know that more seventy thousand Chokora live in Kenya!

Well, we need help so, can you help us? We can work for little money. We're everywhere in Nairobi so, you can see Chokora in every estate in Nairobi and other big cities. As we're nowadays having many babies then we're facing more challenging issues in urban areas where foreign companies are investing our hiding and living sites.

So, what is your problem?

You look like someone with a big stress!

Well, my dear son, I came to Nairobi for help so, I'd take some rest.

I didn't want to shout! If you know how to find a helper at Eastleigh then I'll appreciate it. I've no money to give now so, would you show me somewhere? I want to go to the Somali Small Mall in Eastleigh, and we may get some money over there then I'll give you some money.

According to my believe in Islam, we must support and give something to poor if we can offer it. So, my little son, don't worry! We'll get you some money or food. If you want us to ride a taxi then let me know.

I really don't know how far it's from here.

Is it close to here? Or we'd take the taxi.

We reached the little known Mini-Market at Eastliegh Estate where we bought a big purse and smaller t-shirts. He asked me if I could buy for him some biscuits and a Soda then I bought for him then we met the Mini-Market manager Abdi who gave a nice tour of his complex business.

The Mini-Market manager Abdi told me that the Somali business people are under scrutiny so, he could give her a place to stay at Eastleigh Estate so, I could teach people how to sew and make embroidery items then I disagreed with him because I came to Kenya for a medical treatment.

After disagreeing with his suggestion then I knew that he'd call the Police.

Yes, some are informants to the Kenyan government which gives them a chance to spy for new comers.
I knew many informants because it wasn't my first time to visit Kenya, I came to Kenya in early 1970s for business. I'd not forget what some informants had been doing to us, and they do it everyday. It's business as usual so, I bagged my stuff too quick then I called a taxi so, we'd ride it.

As I was thinking where to go and rent a lodge then I asked the chokora boy then he told me that there are 4 lodges, and the best one is the one which feeds many chokoras who sit in front and backside of the lodge because the Police won't border this lodge, and they don't like to see chokoras.

So, he asked me if I'd rent that lodge.

Then I laughed at him, and I said; let's go there.

I love you, little chokora!

I've not been expecting this offer but it gave me some security concern however; I realized that the little chokora was telling me how safely I could hide at Eastleigh Estate without the fear of police. Then I followed him up to his suggesting lodge then when we've arrived at the lodge.

We entered the lodge to see a receptionist.

Unfortunately, the receptionist was at restroom for taking care little business which we all do.

I asked the chokora boy, where is your hideout? Then he pointed me out. I asked him if they've blankets and mattresses which they can sleep then he laughed at me, and he said; Mama, you must be joking with me. No one dares to bring even outcast items sometimes.

We're all vagabonds!

And you look alike a deportee.

No, little son, I'm not a deportee but I'm a stressed mother who's came to Kenya for help. It was very nice to meet you because you've given me the right opportunity to contemplate exactly what's going on in Kenya? You're very intelligent person so, I really appreciated your help.

I thank you!

As Kenya developed since 1953 then there is still a big problem for security because the Kenyan government relies on informants for information. I came here for a medical treatment now, and I've no money to spend. I wished my relatives in Nairobi for a contribution so, I could cover mys expanses.

I'd not encourage to tell truth while I'm still in Nairobi.

I need the people's help!

Please you can help me so, I can go back to Mogadishu for a refreshed mind. I love my stolen newborn because I didn't' even see his photograph. And nobody is able to tell me how he looked alike! I love my son, and if you can help me then that is the real stress which I've.

So, if you know helpers in Nairobi then please you can share my information with them.

I left the lodge then I wanted to buy some French fries and sandwich at a restaurant between 21sta and 2nd streets in Eastleigh Estate, Nairobi. I met one of my best cousins whom I've not seen for a long time. I greeted her then I asked her how many children she's got? And she replied to me; I've three children.

Did you move to Nairobi? I knew that you used to live in Mombasa.

Yes, I moved to Eastleigh Estate. Have you heard my husband? He's been missing for 7 years. I thought that he married in Kismayo City so, you might have information. I know that I missed you, my cousin. What brought you to Nairobi? I've not been expecting you in Nairobi.

My sister, I lost a newborn!

My cousin, how did you lose the newborn baby? Maybe, someone has stolen your newborn at the hospital so, did you report to the Somali Police?

Yes, I reported to the Somali Police, and they're corrupted for asking bribes which I'd have. I'd be waiting for Gods' help in the near future. I'll soon go back to Mogadishu City so, I'll know if the Somali Police got some information. Where are you going to now? Cousin!

I think that you're going to home, would you mind? If I accompany with you. I'm renting a lodge nearby street children.

Then she responded yes; you can come with me but she asked me how long will I stay in Nairobi? I told her two more day because I wasn't getting a medical treatment for stress

I asked my sister if she learned Amharic then she said to me that she speaks broken Amharic. I didn't understand why she didn't like to learn Amharic. Well, she didn't go to school all her life. As I wanted to welcome her back to Somalia so, I'd encourage her to go to adult school.

My sister told me that she'd not come back to Somalia because she didn't like the same military regime in-charge the county, and she left Somalia after she encountered instability where some government officials threatened her to kill if she exposed what they're doing in Mogadishu City.
She didn't like their crimes!

I've been investigating many issues in Nairobi.

I saw the same crimes in Mogadishu are also going on in Addis Ababa and Nairobi. I don't want to stay in Ethiopia so, I'll be flying to Mogadishu quickly.

My sister invited me to travel with her family to hyena herder who feeds and talk with hyenas. I was so scared to accompany with her to visit the hyena herder.

I didn't know it how to explain but I told my sister that I was planning to go to back Mogadishu.

She accepted my travel to back to home, and she told me that she'd soon visit me when I go back to Mogadishu. I was excited by her announcement.

I called my family in Mogadishu to let them know that my sister will visit us some time so, they must prepare her a vacant room.

Then I bagged my stuff, and I booked a flight ticket to Nairobi.

I farewell my sister, relatives and friends whom I met in Nairobi.

I've flown to Nairobi at 2:00 PM so, I could get some relatives to pick me up at the Aden Abdulle International Airport in Mogadishu City

# Chapter 22

After I landed at the Aden Abdulle International Airport in Mogadishu then I picked up my bag to the Taxi renting hub where I was arrested by the Somali National Security Officers because my bag had Ethiopian ribbon on it.

They immediately labeled me as a spy lady!

Well, I asked them I've a bag which has Ethiopian flag on it then you can call me a spy lady. This is weird so, can I talk to your commander? I'm a Somalian mother who's lost her newborn baby at Banadir Hospital which is run by the Somali Military Regime.

I asked them; did you find my stolen newborn?

Let me be free lady now! Or you'll encounter more problematic issues than asking for me some bribes. I wanted to get out from this uncover taxi. Well, I knew that many people didn't know how taxi drivers were recruited by the Somali National Security Services.

They told me that they'd take me to the Somali National Security Services Headquarters in Mogadishu which is commonly known as the Godka literally meaning the Hole. I couldn't give some bribes then they said to me that if I give them some freeload then they'd release me.

I gave them $ 30!

They dropped me off at Jidka Sodonka literally meaning the 30th Street in Mogadishu.

I wondered why did they pick me up at the Aden Abdulle International Airport? Was it the small Ethiopian flag ribbon on my bag? Or was it something different? I actually couldn't verify why they exactly chose me? Maybe, I look alike spy.

It's very difficult to live in Somalia.

If no salaries are available then it's normal to ask for bribes in third world!

I walked to my home then I first saw my younger child who shouted, and he said, mama is here! Everyone came out and hugged me. Mama, how was the vocation? Have you been enjoying it? How many countries you visited? Tell us!

I told them that I visited Ethiopia and Kenya, and both countries were planning to overthrow the Somali Military Regime so, if you want to live in Mogadishu then there will be a war, and I don't really know when it'll happen.

I'm so scared my children!

Let's me drink some water!

I'll tell you more later.

One of the children asked me if I've some presents from these two countries then I told him that I've no had money to buy presents but my sister had donated to us some presents. I'd only open the luggage bag whenever they're all present.

"He laughed at me," "And he said; Mother, "You're not changing your rules."

I also smiled, I told her to sleep because it was too late, and he was suppose to go school in the morning. He listened to me then he went to his room where he slept quickly without food and milk. I asked later where is the youngest child? Everyone said that he was sleeping.

I told my children, I want to see him.

You need to wake him up now!

They woke up the youngest child of my family, and I said to him, mama, if you can first and foremost choose anything which you may like it then I'd let others share the rest. He laughed at me, and he said to me, I love you very much mother.

I remembered my stolen newborn baby!

And I didn't know how to explain what I was feeling when he said to me, I love you mother. I knew that he'd understand it later in his life then I told my children not tell him that I was still searching the stolen child.

I said to my older children not share information.

I didn't want my child for another stress!

Willing to share wasn't making sense to him so, we'd hide.

Well, mothers know much about how to take care children and bring them up nicely while men go to work and never even wash their clothes even when we're pregnant mothers so, how can we get fair? We must ask for it.

Mothers must get full support whenever they're carrying pregnancies, and every country must legalize to help their women medically and legally. How you think a mother who's lost her child right away after birth? It's really a big shock!

"I couldn't joke with stressed mothers like me."

"I'm still learning many issues in this world day after day." "I've regretted my error," "But it wasn't a good to travel on vocation." I've only been trying to forget the evil incident at the Banadir Hospital where my newborn was stolen.

I returned peacefully however; nothing has changed in Mogadishu City!

Where can I run from these criminal officials?

We're all afraid of this Somali Military Regime, and I can't tell what's the best for all mothers? How should I help others in need? I'm almost recovering from stress that forced to take vocation to abroad. As I told my children, I was interesting to open a women's organization for better social awareness.

Well, when I submitted my application for this women's organization for better social awareness then the Somali Military Government sent to our home some plainclothes policemen to investigate why exactly I wanted to form this organization? I didn't know how to explain it.

Even if I explained well then it's true that the Somali Military Government won't accept it.

We're living in a country where democracy has only been the obedience of the martial law so, we don't know when we'll free to speak and show our feeling to oppose it. Surely, communism, socialism and capitalism are competing how to control Somalia then the rest of Africa.

I love peace!

Let's stop external philosophies.

We can use our customary and constitution for better development, and it's the best time to stop external philosophies in Somalia where they'd not function it well. We must teach our people how grown farms and fish as well as mining.

Yes, I'm telling the truth!

I don't like to waste my time, and I don't watch games. I live to writer or read whenever I've time but it's very hard to enjoy freely in Somalia because the Somali Military Regime wants to make people busy or praise it.

I didn't understand why are they forcing us to praise? They're organized Mafia!

Well, if you want to help me then let's first open a big a house for mothers in Mogadishu City. Fortunately, my rumors reached the Presidential Palace then President H.E. Major-General Mohamed Said Barre ordered to build mother's house in Mogadishu City.

I heard the president's announcement!

I was really excited then I thought that I'd be able to visit and enjoy in this mother's house then I remembered that only members of the Somali elite could go there. I didn't digest how things were going on in the country.

Let's wish the best for mothers around the world.

I'm still suffering from the stress after many years, and there are no tips to who's stolen my newborn boy?

*Dr. Badal Kariye*

So, we're still living under a corrupted martial which foreign powers with various philosophical ideologies are still funding technically, financially and militarily.

I'll get justice soon!

## Chapter 23

Yesterday was history and today is struggling while I don't know tomorrow so, can the Somali Military Regime help me to find the stolen newborn? I doubt it, they're all crazy and corrupted officials who only ask for money. I don't hate them but I sometimes decline to say yes for bribes.

Every job depends to be done with some bribes.

If I didn't lose my stolen child then I'd have never learned what was going on in Somalia? It's true that most people know too much when they seek for information and services available to the general public. I'd not came back to insult this corrupted martial law anyhow; we must say no to orders if it violates our basic rights.

I know that we also blame to the Commander-in-Chief for everything!

He's only one person so, can we ask ourselves the truth? We're doing the crimes which we normally blame to the superiors in-charge. Willingly, I love the truth but many people prefer to support their nomadic customary so, we can't tell who is right? Who is wrong? I don't know it.

I'm confused with these lies in the country!

I went to the Somali Police Headquarters which is literally known as Escola Policia to get some information regarding to my stolen newborn baby at Banadir Hospital for many years ago then when I reached the front gate of the the Somali Police Headquarters where I met Officer Hareey.

He urgently recognized me, and he said to me that the the Somali Police and the Central Investigation Department "CID" were still working on my case but there were no leads on it yet. He was very happy to see after couple of years, and he said to me that he was full colonel in-charge the Banadir Regional Police Command.

I thought that I was luck to know him well!

However; whether you're a low or high ranking officer, there is always need for bribes because the salary wasn't enough to cover personal costs, and most of them use drugs like Khat & wine after daily work in the country. It's true that we're 100% Muslim but we're not religious.

If you're very religious then there has been a possibility which you might not get rank promotions because the Somali Military Regime has been using and placing us into various world ideologies which conflicted our nomadic customary & ethnics so, it's wise to act fool in Somalia.

You can't show how smart are you? It's the truth!

Well, the Somali Military Regime asked for volunteers to teach Somali language to rural dwellers which encouraged many people to come and immigrate to bigger towns in the country then they faced with lack of jobs then they turned to join the only revenue generating resource which was the military.

Well, it is true that if people can get jobs then it is easy for them to join the military where they can learn many things including how kill or earn money without fear.

Or we'll force other to give up our stolen and illegally transferred lands by the corrupted colonialists to Ethiopia and Kenya.

We're not cowards to fight and show mission to reclaim our lands!

Well, the issue for greater Somalia was morally high at all costs within the Somali Military Regime which called itself later the Somali Democratic Republic.

Surely, they couldn't tell me where is my stolen baby? So, how money times did they tell me about greater Somalia? As I compared their visionary mission to combat and stop the illegal mastermind of colonialists for making Africa and many other places as conflict stricken and invested then I I couldn't say stop.

I was very sympathetic for greater Somalia!

Truly, one thing which the Somali Military Regime claimed legally was how to revive the defense strategy which Somalia could claim its territories legally and militarily, Somalia beat Ethiopia fully and confidently without the support of the so-called Western world or other opposing countries to the Western world's activities in the Horn of Africa.

After Somalia won clearly the Somalia-Ethiopia conflict for the disputed territory of Ogadenia then the Western world and the other opposing countries requested to Somalia for urgent withdrawal. It was true that Ethiopia even hired mercenary men and women from various countries as historians documented and mentioned in several newspapers and journals.

So, I asked myself why are they not fighting to get my stolen newborn baby? Well, he's also a Somalian!

As no one has even came with an answer then I went to Hamarweyne Market which was once the biggest market in Mogadishu City in order to some food and clothes then I stopped a taxi for a ride. Though, I've money to give the Taxi driver then He said to me that he saw my photo on the Somali National Television which I requested for my stolen child.

He offered me free ride to Hamarweyne Market.

After I got off his taxi then he told me that he was working as an undercover agent with the Somali National Security Services. Surely, I've not shocked because I knew how they're working in Mogadishu City. He even told my case file number, and who was really working on it? I loved to listen to him.

He offered me if he could give me some money that I personally declined because it's possible for us that others following up his daily movement could incriminate him so, I rejected his offer then I walked away then he thanked me for the cooperation and accepting his ride.

He said to me; goodbye mama!

I entered Hamarweyne Market where I wanted to buy some gold, food and clothes for the children. I first headed to the gold department so, I could get two sets of modern gold because I wanted to restore it for the future wide of my stolen son as the best wish.

Many people might think that I was crazy however; it's always wise to wish the best even for those who passed away before us so, why not a stolen one? I love him! If I get him back then I'll do everything to please him however; I'm not sure how long it will take for me to see him again?

I'll wish all the best for him.

I bought the two gold sets then I headed to the food department where I want to buy food then they're selling too expensive more than Bakaraha Market. I noticed that there were foreigners who shopped well with high currencies, and that is why I couldn't buy the same money as Bakaraha Market? So, there is no official price set!

I then walked to the clothes department which has also astonished me. I asked myself if I was living in abroad or not. What's going on in Hamarweyne Market? Well, are the only rich people able to buy something in Hamarweyne Market? Where is the Somali Military Regime? Let's tell them to set up prices.

Well, if the Somali Military Regime is trying to advocate for a greater Somalia then why can't they set up prices for commodities? I'm actually interesting in to see how they'd fix local issues before we think the broader vision for a greater Somalia. I love my country but I see a bunch of crooks are still mislead the public.

I hate to lie!

After I completed my shopping then I headed to the Bus Stop but I saw many things were wrong in the Hamarweyne Market therefore; I asked some people if the government was trying to rebuild the Clothing Department which was locally known as Ba'adlaha section after fire has completely burnt and demolished the rusty and corrugated metal stores.

Well, one lady cried badly, and she said to me that she was the only one support her family, and the only place which they earn for income has widely burnt so, she wanted me to give her something. I was shocked how easily people could become beggars? I noticed carefully her motions then I gave her twenty thousand Somali shillings.

She thanked to me, and she wished me the best!

"I've not told her that I was also having some problems because it could knock her off." I asked her if the Somali Military Government was planning to rebuild their Ba'adlaha Clothing Department then she said to me that she couldn't tell the unseen, and she wasn't relying on them.

She didn't like the endless corruptions with the Somali Military Government!

I apologized her!

As I was walking through Hamarweyne Market then two gamblers stopped me for a gambling play then they first offered free game trail because they wanted to know if I could show them some money but they realized me that I've no money. They said to me that they wanted to know where I put my money so, they could either steal or snatch even I didn't play the game.

I told these gamblers that I was veteran so, I knew their tricks and how they like to trap innocent people? One of the gamblers said to me that I've been clever for many years then he returned to me my little purse which he stole right away when they stopped me for the game.

And he said to me; we're veteran thugs!

We're not joking with you, and we noticed that you've had problems!

Have nice day mama!

Well, it's not only in Somalia where you can get corrupted people acting like that but we can even them in every society. I boarded on to the bus to Bakaraha area where I used to live.

People are talking about government corruptions on the bus!

I got out from the bus then I called someone to help me carry my load.

He helped me until we reached in front of my house then he asked me if I got back my stolen baby then I replied to him, no, I didn't get my child. I'll wait for the Somali Military Regime to give me a fully detailed report or they'll have to find my stolen newborn at the Banadir Hospital.

I love my child!

## Chapter 24

I woke up early in the morning in order to some fresh kidneys and livers from the butchery nearby my home where I saw the man which the Somali National Security Services shot a thief who's been harassing people for many years, and this time I realized how even the martial law wasn't working for every citizen.

I asked one of the ladies if he'd a knife or a gun before they shot him then she replied to me that she wasn't present when they exactly shot him. I've not asked for questions then I watched how ruthlessly they took the dead body throwing him int to the back of Land Rover pick-up.

Regarding to my analysis for bribes in the country, I knew that more killings will be easy soon.

We've no civil courts!

If you look alike as an opponent then the Somali Military Regime may arrest or even kill you so, why would I risk my life? I've not been fool. I always said that I love the country and its regime because my safety relied on to follow up their wish to obey martial law at all cost.

Well, if they couldn't find my stolen child then there is no reason to obey its dirtier martial law in Somalia, and it's possible for people to challenge and even overthrow them. They're not deserving to lead Somalia's leadership which has been suffocating the people in every region.

We must oppose this corrupted leadership!

"People aren't fools to accept more crimes against humanity in Somalia."

We've no money to campaign how to overthrow this corrupted martial government however; I can have ideas to propagate so, people should know the truth, and they'll organize a grassroots in order to overthrow it more diplomatically than demonstrators so that we could win the true war.

As I'm not politically illiterate how they conducted such direct and unlawful assassinations publicly? Well, I noticed when the Somalia's Death Squad attacked one of my neighbors who's done nothing wrong. We're shocked by their noise which the villagers couldn't sleep.

Let's campaign to stop such crimes!

If we always think that we can't stop then who will work for us to stop their crimes? I want every to organize the grassroots so, we can show some resistance to your heinous crimes for asking bribes to do their official work.

Running away isn't a solution to this internal public issue so, if they can secure the safety of ordinary citizens then why should w give taxes to this military region? We need to say something before it's too late.

Everyone knows what crimes are going on in our beloved country.

*Dr. Badal Kariye*

As you know that many current official grew up during the Somali Military Revolution so, they adapted to work for bribes under the shadowy imperialism of foreign based ideologies which contradicted our religious dogma.

If I asked them where is my stolen newborn baby? Surely, no one has leading information from the Somali Police Headquarters and the Somali National Security Services so, are they only busy to abuse innocent people? Well, it looks alike the truth is like delusion in Somalia.

Can we tell them to stop crimes? No, because everyone is afraid to face punishment which is possible to loose some of his limps or life so, I think that there was no one who came forward to say stop your crimes, we've had enough so, we didn't want to flee from Somalia for seeking total refuge.

Frogs are not here to damage!

I morally disagreed with the Death Squad how they shot innocent man then they placed him a note which was written that the dead man was a longtime thief whom they've been searching many years in the area. Well, I could tell that he was politically assassinated when they noticed that he was organizing various local gangs to work with the rebellious factions within the Somali clans.

How many people they murdered without court trial? Thousands of innocent people were murdered in the Northern and South Central regions by the Somali Military Regime in order to stay in power and reduce force's capabilities before they turned to overthrow longtime Leader of the Martial Law.

I love the facts!

I entered the Butchery then I asked him if he'd some goat meat. He said to me that they closed down business today because his brother was murdered meaninglessly. He wasn't glad to sell meat because he'd a condolence to take care so, he was waiting for the Somali National Security Services to call him so, he'd get his brother's body from the Mogadishu City Mortuary.

I wanted to follow him to the Mogadishu City Mortuary then I asked him; he said to me that he was willing people to accompany him because he was afraid of the Somali National Security Services which they'd easily incriminate him for crimes that he's never committed.

Yes, mama, you can follow me to be witness!

Let's go to the Mogadishu City Mortuary.

We went to the Mogadishu City Mortuary where we tried to recover the dead man's body then we're surprised when we saw a receipt on the dead man's body. We asked them what is this? Surely, you killed this man then you're looking for money for giving us his body.

Are you joking with us?

No, we're not joking with you, and if you can't pay money then we can even kill you too!

Go away! You can only come back with the money!

We're truly astonished how stupid were they? Even there is a corruption at the Mogadishu City Mortuary so, where can we escape?

I told the Butcher that there should be a time in the near future which this corrupted martial law wouldn't work so, he'd be patient to accept whatever he encounters in this dying nation. He accepted my warning then we returned to Bakaraha Market where he re-opened his butchery.

He started selling meat with less price to many people who were waiting for him to return then he asked to everyone for organizing a demonstration on next Friday after Friday prayers. As everyone was very suspicious about what he was asking for then I jumped in to explain to them.

Because we must encourage our people how to stop criminals like the ones who shot innocent man then they labeled him that he was criminal gang whom they've been searching him for many year. It wasn't true but it was one of their carefully planned lies to cover up their illegal crimes against innocent civilians.

As we knew the truth about this case then we couldn't talk about it publicly.

He gave me more 7 Kilograms of meat then I told him that I'd be a witness if he files a lawsuit against his brother's killers. I gave him my home telephone. I also told him that I've been searching my stolen newborn baby. I missed him for many years, and still the martial law has done nothing to help me.

I'm still waiting for help too!

My country is still facing new challenges which I couldn't stop or help to change for a good governance.

I talked about the on-going instability and lack of effective security in the country then I'd be public enemy number one. Thereby; we must talk to share the truth no matter what would happen in the near future? They can't be above the law but they've been acting as if they're above the martial law itself.

Well, we're afraid of the Somali Military Regime to plan other heinous crime in Somalia if they seemed to lose more territory to the various rebellious groups. I'd rather flee from the country before they infected me their nepotism disease which has never had a treatment.

It's very complex issue to talk about the Somali Military Regime and its failures.

"We're not swimming in the dirtier pool of uncertainty in national politics."

I've to get justice for all!

We need justice for all, and we must get it now.

*Dr. Badal Kariye*

Affirmatively, we obey the martial law but it's bringing for good fortunes so, we must get rid of it before it steaks or kills more innocent people in this rich countryside. I mean if we can overthrow them too. Goodbye butcher!

## Chapter 25

I wanted to invite the plainclothes officers who were working on my case then I called the Mogadishu Police Headquarters where a police lady answered my call. She asked me, what do you need for extra help? Well, if you don't have extra issue. Please you can the Police tomorrow.

No alerts now to document!

Please you can call the Police tomorrow then she hugged up the call. I was shocked how she hanged my call? I thought that we've a functioning system in the country, and we'll see tomorrow if they tell something when I call him back. Surely, they'll do the same thing. Maybe, she'll hanged up.

Business is out of order nowadays!

I worked hardly to earn my family's daily living in Mogadishu City.

Well, I'll know that if there will solutions soon.

I went to Lido Beach for family swimming but there were many foreigners who'd been swimming and relaxing on Lido Beach. My husband drove us over there. We're good swimmers but we've not had swimming equipments so, we rented some swimming equipments from swimming store.

After renting some swimming equipments then we headed to the beach so, we can enter sea and swim by using our rented swimming equipments. One of my children requested me to rent the sea motorcycle then we told him that we've no had extra money.

We love Lido Beach!

I didn't reject it for him however; we should encourage to rent the best and safety assured sea equipments only. It's not bee wise to advice him right way but he understood us before we further explained to him then we started swimming until the sun set down. We're enjoyed swimming well!

It was a nice day for my family to swim together but I'm afraid that these foreigner will take our beach in the near future as they're illegally investing to enjoy without taxation. Well, if the Somali Military Regime has been corrupting everything then we should know the fact that they only benefiting from the corrupted martial law.

We know it well.

Africans think better whenever they feel hungry but we can farm or look after our livestock nowadays, and surely, most white people assumed that Africans are inferior race than white race however; it's all based on greedy philosophy.

I believe that all humans are equal, they must have equal basic rights unfortunately, if and when our African people understands the true criminals then we tend to not expose it because we're still following up the wrong food steps.

*Dr. Badal Kariye*

See how these foreigners are nowadays enjoying at Lido Beach and other Somali beaches across the country.

We're not sure for it what was going on? We came out from the sea because one lady shouted that she saw a shark then we all came out from the sea. She was eaten by some sea animal but it wasn't a big sea animal so, we're not sure what was the problem? I couldn't know the truth.

We love Lido Beach!

Living nearby Lido Beach is wonderful, is it? My younger son said to me, we love to swim at Lido Beach.

People from Somalia and around the world love to come and visit Lido Beach however; they came to drink wing and smoke drugs. "We all love to enjoy it." Had we been enjoying it for many years? Yes, but the Somali Military Regime didn't care to collect rubbish and other harmful wastage.

I couldn't mention more nasty issues!

We're not certainly willing to give up our precious assets.

Have they stolen anything? If we've not shown kindness then they'd not come to visit us and spend their vocation in Mogadishu City. I came to show my family how they've got a better beach to swim and enjoy without fear and restrictions. They're welcome! I want to share every mother how to protect and save children from thugs.

Because one of my youngest sons was stolen at the Banadir Hospital after I delivered him, and he's been missing in stealing since 1977 until now on. I got no powerful supporters in Somalia, and my family members are not serving the Somali Military Regime so, we're a poor and helpless family.

Let's keep our Lido Beach clean!

Yes, we can save people and the environment too.

There are winners and losers in every nation, and we're part of these nations.

Somalia is our country so, we'd enjoy better than foreigners but the Somali Military Government has been fighting against corruption, nepotism and illiteracy since 1969 until 1980, and after 1980s people addicted to a disease of nomadic tribalism into urbanized cities like Mogadishu Metropolitan.

As I knew that there were still more crimes, and we must for ethics committee to deal with local and foreigners who're violating our blue laws and the constitution. I worried about our youth to come and enjoy at Lido Beach where they may enter to see couple of foreigners seducing or doing immoral movements.

We're Islamic nation! However; we're truly confused with foreign ideologies which the corrupted Military Government implemented to base on us locally, and we can only talk about it externally.

That isn't right.

We returned to my home then we sat at the dinning room for open discuss to talk and share experiences which they liked at Lido Beach. We couldn't conform our lifestyle without Lido Beach so, who want to go there every Friday so, they enjoy and swim around this best beach.

Do you love the Lido Beach? Yes, we love it.

Are we ready to defend our country? Let's stop this Corrupted Military Regime.

We've plenty of resources in Somalia.

I didn't insult people who's even asked for me bad questions? So, why are we not telling these foreigner how to behave quietly? We love Lido Beach so, we must save our people and protect the environment willy-nily. It's wise to so! If foreigners wants to obey with the martial law then we welcome too.

All foreigners must obey the martial law!

Justice is for all so, if the foreigners came in legally with visas then they can enjoy and travel throughout country. But we must make sure that they don't steal children or try to adopt without legality so, we must know everything before they do it in our beloved country.

That is truth! We're a strong nation in Africa but we can't save our children from criminals and other thugs.

I want to get back my stolen child!

Well, the children are the flowers of the future!

"We've condoned to many families," "And someone is missing everyday." If you confront the Somali Military Regime then you'll be counted as one of the missing in action. So, I'm acting smart to do my own business.

If you can't help others then let's be silent!

We saw many innocents are locked behind unknown penitentiary camps in Mogadishu City where majority of people can't track down innocents. Only few soldiers knew these unknown penitentiary camps so, I don't want to enter and die there in.

Please I'll only wait for my stolen child if and whenever they bring him back or if they get a leading information to track down whoever has already stolen him. I'm not the mother who's suffering from such problematic stress.

It's hard to easily enjoy in Somalia if this corrupted martial law strives in the near future anyhow;

*Dr.Badal Kariye*

I believe that it'd soon collapse then we'll inherit chaotic and anarchic problems which can lead this beloved nation into civil war for the control of power and tribal fame.

“We'll see it soon.”

# Chapter 26

I've already realized many public servants started joining with the rebellious factions from several Somali clans who had decided to overthrow our Somali Military Government then I knew that my pending case shouldn't be solved one way of the other because we're having slipping nations.

Unfortunately, if some public servants didn't get money they used to get promotional ranks however; if they reached last promotional ranks then nothing had changed from what they're complaining about? They either decided to join with the rebellious factions from several Somali clans mainly the Somali Salvation Democratic Front (SSDF), the Somali National Movement (SNM) and the United Somali Congress (USC).

The trust and the truth opened new possibilities!

Many people including public servants fed up with the various trickery tactics of the dying once military mighty then they either joined with these tribally founded factions or fled from Somalia to Arab countries where they seek for a refuge and odd jobs.

As a mother and laborer, I was confused with national issues because I knew that how silly we're in the countryside? Maybe, it could occur in Mogadishu City too. There was a fear of tribal and ethnic cleansing though which many innocent people will suffer from.

Well, I needed to get back my stolen child! Had I got mission to stop such propaganda from the Somali clans? No, because I wasn't that rich to bail out!

It's not too late for some people who went to Arab countries earlier before the Somali clans completely overthrow the corrupted Somali military regime because everything collapses unknowingly and emotionally with the favoritism of the illegally organized tribal factions.

Most ordinary people who wanted to go to abroad liked countries like Saudi Arabia, Egypt, Iraq, Omen and Dubia where they used to get odd jobs for survival until the country went into civil war.

Who started the civil war? Certainly, the various tribal factions who'd no political plan to use and government the country after they ousted longtime military dictator and President H.E. Mohamued Said Barre out of Mogadishu City.

Finally, the warring tribal factions trained in Ethiopia and Kenya began advancing towards Mogadishu City after they captured Baidao town then many of the tribally armed militias in Mogadishu City attacked the Somali Presidential Palace which is locally known as Villa Somalia.

Within few days of heavy fighting in Mogadishu City then the Somali Military Regime gave up to fight in Mogadishu City after they realized that these tribally armed militias weren't giving up the fight for freedom of nowhere then Somalia went into more chaotic and anarchic civil war.

Who're responsible for the civil war?

Truly, the Somali Military Regime, the tribal factions, the Manifesto Group who're tribal old politicians and the Somali traders because they're the four major players who've been lobbying for the total control of national leadership thus; I understood that I'd get back my stolen child.

So, it was another challenge to face then I told my children to flee from Mogadishu City to Nairobi Kenya then one of my children told me that we'd be okay because we're not politicians or government employees. What didn't he understand? The tribalism which wasn't curable disease!

I asked my husband to refuel our cars so, if anything new comes then we'll run wherever people should be fleeing then the two warring tribal factions who overthrew the Somali Military Regime changed political dynamics into tribal politics then the war had a new face for many clans.

I cried when I heard heavy artillery & other weapons used to cross fire in Mogadishu City!

I knew that no more Somalia standing as a government for more than decades because it signified my dream which I'd once before. Thousands of innocent people died within 6 months in Mogadishu City so, who was responsible? The Western world and their opponents who've both been confusing the Somali Military Regime.

I knew that it'd take a longtime for Somalis to understand what they've been doing in their country after they beautified our neighboring countries. Wisely, I'd take my children out Mogadishu City because it's too risk to live in a war zone like the world war I & II.

We bagged our stuff then we drove our cars into the Afgoi-Kismayo road!

As we're driving though the Afgoi-Kismayo road then we met many people who'd also fed from the on-going cross artillery and weaponry fighting then we stopped at Afgoi District where most of the Somalis used to come on vocation but now it was like a refugee camp.

People robbed people, people raped people, people killed people and people ran away for their lives because the majority of the Somali people in Mogadishu City who fled from the tribal civil war never knew about the real issue for the cross fight among the three warring factions which had already succeed to depose the Somali Military Regime. Everyone was somehow confused!

After one and half day on the Afgoi-Kismayo road when we arrived in Kismayo City where some of our relative lived in over centuries then we offloaded our parcel from the cars unfortunately, we're told that there would be another fighting in Kismayo City between two of Somalia's most corrupted clans.

After 3 days the fight broke out in Kismayo City then we loaded our stuff. We headed to a unconventional road which was known as Jidka Habar Walid literally meaning "the Parental Cured Road." It was one of the toughest roads we even traveled through because it was a rainy season and mud made many cars to stuck in while people feared both sides of the waring factions might came after them to loot, rape and kill them.

Everybody was scared!

As we're traveling through the Jidka Habar Walid literally meaning "the Parental Cured Road," more 14 days because whenever a car stuck in the road then they'd pull it out so, other cars could safely bypass therefore; our daily menu became the wildlife which we hunted for food.

When I reached Liboi Somalia safely then we unpacked our cars. We built a wooden huts to live in however; the water was too hard to drink and salted. We suffered from diarrhea for three consecutive days before the Medicine Sans Frontier brought oral rehydration solution (ORS), Malaria drugs and food mainly porridge

After 7 days then the same tribal factions started fight to control drinking wells in Liboi town then they started to use heavy weapons then a majority of fleeing people fled from Liboi Somalia into Liboi Kenya where the United Nations High Commission for Refugees granted them refugee status and protection.

Then we entered the Liboi Kenya Refugee Camp!

Well, I can still tell you that the Liboi Kenya refugee camp had one of the world's best UNHCR coordinators, and his name was sakawaden whom we still consider to meet him and thank him for doing extraordinary job in deadly environment where various armed gangs came in to rob, rape or kill opponents.

Special thanks to the UNHCR coordinator Saqawaden for providing full security and distribute food even during the night on your UNHCR Nissan pick-up car. We will always wish you all the best for your future. Your willing aspiration encouraged to understand life and its circumstances.

After 1994 the Liboi Kenya refugee camp was closed down by the UNHCR then were' transferred to Dhagahley Refugee Camp where we stayed until 1994 then we moved to Nairobi in 1995. After knowing how life was harder than our previously closed down Liboi Kenya Refugee Camp then it forced us to move out to Nairobi for a better job,education and life.

Somalia was at war with its people!

## Chapter 27

Moving out as refugees from Dagahley Refugee Camp in the North Eastern Province into Nairobi Kenya in 1995 wasn't a great surprise because I've dreamed it before when I noticed that the Somali people had been fed up with their martial law in-charge for everything. I knew that one day we'd flee from Somalia for tribal civil war.

It's true that some tribal factions wanted to make the country as messy as the carcass massacre it'd been suffering from since 1991 until 1995, and Somalia still suffers from chaotic and anarchic tribalism that refuels atrocities in the country where every warring tribe wants to grab the national leadership without consensus.

"Well, we're luck to came and live in Nairobi."

Millions fled from Somalia because of the tribal civil war which was organized by the rebellious tribal factions who were funded and militarily supported by many nations in our neighbors and third parties from the international community. As Somali Military Government has completely collapsed then Somali tribal factions hadn't alternative political plan to save the nation.

People fled from Somalia into the same three neighboring countries with Somalia who funded, armed and trained the Somali rebellious factions in order to crush the Somali Military Government which has been enjoying the supreme mighty in the Horn of Africa and Africa at large.

So, I became hopeless to for the search of my stolen newborn baby in Somalia!

This was one of the bad dreams I've ever had to tell people but when I told many of my neighbors then they agreed with me because everyone wanted the martial law to end, and let's elect civil and democratic president after longtime they're were in-charge day to day activities in the country.

Having traveled into many rough and riskier roads in Somalia and Kenya, we finally came to live the Capital City of Kenya - Nairobi as our second home. It's true that the Kenyan people are generously very kind to live with but the Kenyan Police was one oft he worse government entities who harassed innocent Somali refugees for asking bribery to release them after they handcuffed.

I've never had problems with the Kenyan Police but when they captured my grown kids then I was suppose to get some money to bribe them in order to release my detained grown children. It was a common thing to happen once and while in Nairobi and other bigger cities in Kenya.

Well, if Kenyan Police stop you then they'd first ask for a Kenyan National Identity Card which is locally known Kitampulisho Cha Taifa. If you're a Kenyan Somali then you must have one if not then you must pay them bribes since 1991 until now.

So, it's a common practice!

So, I didn't know what we would achieve in the future! “Wishing the best is always okay with my family.”

So, I and my children came here in Nairobi to work and survive however; we knew that we'd encounter life challenging issues in Nairobi however; it was now better than to live Mogadishu City where warlords controlled everything. Many Somalis set up small businesses at Eastleigh Estate in Nairobi.

For today's reality! Eastleigh Estate in Nairobi became the biggest trading market for Eastern and Central Africa, and it generates more than $ 5.7 billion sales annually. So, the Somalis had also employed more Kenyans as well as training them how to do business and trade it.

Well, Somali Businesses located at Eastleigh State is five times more than any businesses going on in Kenya.

We loved to strive through such on-going business developments at Eastleigh Estate where we opened our small shop that had been supporting our family since 1995 until 2006. We still love Kenyan people but foreign entities wants to create more crisis among Kenyans and Somalis.

Because the corrupted imperialists won't like to see Africans who understood each to work and do business as usual thus; the colonialists would always want to implement plans which Africans hate each other so, they may easily steal and benefit from the plentiful of the Africa's natural resources.

Verily, some African leaders are now fed up the direct and indirect dictation of their former colonialists, and they're not teaching people how to defend and preserve their true identities from invading forces to steal their natural resources once way or the other.

So, we're not worried about Somalia!

Somali leaders and warlords were paid enough to destroy Somali Military Regime when they rejected the Western world to drill oil and gas in Somalia where they suggested to take away 65% while they only offered 35% to the Somali People and its military regime in-charge.

As the Western governments failed Plan A then they didn't succeed Plan B because they thought that they'd easily control the armed Somali tribal militias so, they could sign a bogus contract deals for oil drilling in Somalia which turned into more bloody civil war.

Who was behind internal conflicts? Not Somalis! It's best time to let Somalis that we invested another nation while we're still destroying our homeland.

Wake up Somalis!

We mustn't rely on establishing businesses in every country we're living in but we must send our children to schools so, they get the best education for better management and leadership in the near future when we finally return to our our homeland - Somalia.

As we're not returning soon to our homeland - Somalia then it's always better for us to go back when the situation permits however; if we return while majority of us got the best education then I'm positive that the we can once again lead Africa and the rest oft he world.

If you don't know the true history of the Somali people please let me summarize that Somalis had the first kingdom which was named Diiftire Kingdom from the Tanade Darod clan, and it was overthrown by the Ajuran Kingdom that was formed later, and it was hired by other Somali clans mainly from Darod clans in order to discard the Diiftire Kingdom because this Diiftire Kingdom was very harsh to use justice & resources as means to oppress other clans so, if you want to know the reality of history in Somalia then you can search and look into Greek Archives, Turkish Ottoman Archives as well as the Chinese Archives for Dynasties.

Somalis went into different wars such as Ahmed Gurey war against Abyssinia, Said Abdulle Hassan war against British imperialists etc. And they normally rise up to win many times so, I've no doubt that we'll win in the near future but we must educate our people so, they can lead us as they've once led the rest of Africa and the world at large. We're proud to be Somalians!

I and my children were luck to flee from the civil war so, we'd live in Kenya for survival peacefully until Somalis stops the civil war and they form a government that represents the common interests of the ordinary citizens. We love Somalia to resurrect itself without third party interests.

It is very ridiculous to let our neighbors to form a government for Somalia because they're the ones who funded, armed and trained Somali rebellious tribal factions in their respective countries since 1978 until now, and they're the ones who destroyed Somalia's mighty.

So, they only want to establish a puppet government which has no military capabilities to stop their direct and indirect dictations to our daily affairs, and they've been arming various tribal factions in Somalia since the civil war broke out until now no.

I really don't know when these neighboring countries will stop violations of the Somali Sovereignty, the Charters of the United Nations, the Principles of the International law. Well, we normally see crimes happen but we don't see the real solutions between Ethiopia and Somalia as well as Kenya and Somalia.

Because the colonialists left Africa and many other places around the world a demonic puzzle for problematic cross border demarcations so, it'd not easy to solve territorial disputes, and why the colonialists did such heinous crimes of cross border confusions? It's dive rule and steal the natural resources of others wisely!

Wake up Somalis! Wake up Africans! Wake up the innocent world!

I've never thought that Somalis should accept Ethiopia and Kenya to form a puppet government each to control Somalia directly or directly however; it's possible for some Somali traitors to accept and do something wrong when they think that their tribe can only rule the rest of the country for enjoying public resources.

Let's help Somalia as Somalis!

# Chapter 28

On September 20 2013 I and my children had immigrated to the United States of America under the U.S. Refugee Resettlement Program. I thought that American offers many opportunities but we faced another tough life for struggling survival.

It's true that we arrived into the land of opportunities but we didn't know how to benefit it thereby we started to get help from the local social welfare center for food stamp and some pocket money which we used to buy stuff.

We're glad to come to America!

As I'm the mother, I didn't know more about America and I was too old to learn English. I started asking for where is my stolen newborn? Is he alive? Or Is he died? I've never told my children that there was a child who was stolen at the Banadir Hospital.

Because I didn't want my children to suffer from the same stress that has been confusing me for many years but it's true that when you're too old then you've the responsibility to share family information and resources.

I loved all my kids!

After staying few months in Sandiego, California then we moved out to Minnesota State where we've been living in since 2007, and we're all now naturalized American citizens who're part of the American dream.

It was very hard to old person like to catch with the American dream however; my children' had simply catch with the American dream while I've still been suffering from the stress that shocked when someone had intentionally stolen my newborn baby.

It's wise to share the truth!

I invited all my children one day, and we told them that there was a newborn boy who was stolen at Banadir Hospital in Mogadishu City, and it's possible for us search him in the near future. As your mother, I didn't know who has stolen him? We must search together now.

If you want to know how many years your father and I had been search for him? Then he was older than Badal! Do you have question? If you don't have questions then everyone can start searching for him

I told you the truth!

I knew that your father didn't like to share the truth however; I love him the same way I love everyone of you, dear children, I've had bad and good days in my life so, if you find your brother even after my death then please you tell him how deeply I loved him.

This stress won't leave me until death or finding him alive.

*Dr. Badal Kariye*

If you meet a great adviser then you can ask for questions and answers as you're gaining from the wisdom which he or she may breath whenever mouth opens however; some people may talk and never listen to elders.

It's a common mistake among human being!

# Chapter 29

Life in America was easy to every race and religion before September 11, 2001 when terrorists attacked the World Trade Center in New York unfortunately, many innocent Muslims blamed for something they never knew about it.

As media outlets spread propaganda and scary tactics to suffocate American Muslims then many untold secrets exposed, and the American people are still learning to know who attacked them? Fortunately, we knew that many innocent lives died or wounded however; we"re still know who really tried Al-Qadea leader?

Well, as the American President Barack Obama announced that they killed the Al-Qadea Leader Osama Bin Laden then why can't he tell us who's been recruiting young Somalis from various states in the United State of America?

I'm truly scared for my children!

There are recruiting people in America so, it's the best time for tracking down and arresting them before they recruit innocent young people to terrorism activities around the world. We can't watch anymore to listen to various media outlets defaming our immigrant communities.

It's not fair what sometimes media outlets broadcast however; every parent has obligation to ask and monitor their children, and if they see something wrong then they can contact to the local Law Enforcement Agencies for further help.

I'm sure that the Law Enforcement Agencies will you legally, and stop your children traveling without your knowledge possibly.

So, if you see something wrong with a child or children then you can inform the Nearest Law Enforcement Agency.

If you don't tell something to the Nearest Law Enforcement Agency about your child or children who wants to join with various local gangs as well as the international terrorists then there is no way to get help after they travel to terrorism occupied zone around the globe.

Well, most of the immigrant community knew that their young children have no play grounds to play or other games to enjoy whenever they're free from school, and there are lack of enough jobs to work whenever there is an economic downgrade.

It's very touchy issue to address such social disparities among immigrant communities across the United State of America, and we must address social development collaboratively and understandably so, we can survive together in a prosperous America.

I wish that our government will help the various immigrant communities for social development and reintegration programs so, everyone can win daily bread in America.

Let's work together!

*Dr. Badal Kariye*

Having angry with others and showing your resent won't solve your problematic issues so, if you're dealing with mankind then be nice to them even if they're nice to you. It's wise to help people in need so that you'll get it in turn.

Maybe, I'll soon get extra support.

By the way, let's try to help one another so, others may follow us to help and support others in need.

In martial law, we couldn't speak it!

How about the civil war? Well, it's even worse than martial law 99.9%!

We deeply regretted what's been going on in Somalia since 1960s until now,and we're profoundly sorry to know that there is a government in Somalia which was based on Somali power sharing clan formula locally known as 4.5 which is not justice.

There is nothing call 4.5 Somali power sharing clan formula that was formed by the Somali clans however; it's illegal invention from third political parties who're not happy to see Somalis enjoy as one nation, one language and have the best and the everlasting religion - Islam in the world.

Please we need to think well, and we must help others in need.

I love you Somalis, and Somali mothers must force their husbands, brothers, fathers and sons to lay down weapons and take the pen to complete with the rest of the world.

Please you better understand me as a mother, wife, sister & woman who wants you to succeed in your nation then we can try to help the world peacefully and wisely.

Put down the guns!

No one could win the war with guns locally, regionally and globally!

“It's true that we all need peace.”

# Chapter 30

I and my children thanked to the American people and the United State of America for giving us the hope to immigrate and be part of the United State of America. I couldn't thank all enough however; I really appreciated how many people supported my family.

I knew America before when two Peace Corps employee narrated me a lot about the American lifestyle anyhow; we're now living in America as a naturalized American citizens, and we're truly proud of it whether you like it or not.

Finally, we resettled peacefully without fear of persecution, race or religion in America.

I'm still suffering from my stress, and I won't be fine until I see my stolen newborn boy. Please if you can help me then let's try to search and find my stolen newborn baby because that is the only solution and treatment for my stress.

I've no money to search him!

I wish that God will bring him to me one day!

We love to welcome everyone who can help us search and find him, and if you know someone that has had a child who was stolen at Banadir Hospital? Please you can contact to my family and the writer of this book and many other books so, we can reunite with our stolen newborn boy.

Surely, the stealing of the newborn boy made my mother to suffer from a recent stroke as she began to think about him more and more everyday, and I wish him to come and join with us before she passes away.

On behalf of my family and our beloved mother, please if you know our stolen child or you've ever came across someone saying hearsay about a stolen child at Banadir Hospital in Mogadishu then you can contact my family in Somalia or around the world.

We're not relinquishing for the search of our stolen newborn boy until we get him alive or know him as dead person.

I told my children to learn, achieve and be part of America! Because I'm not expecting for quicker solutions to their original homeland which broke many patriotic hearts since 1991 until now, and I don't really know when Somalia will resurrect and be part of the international community.

And it's the best time to stop your media propaganda because the American people are fed up with your lies and illegal accusations against innocent people while you can't talk about who really trained terrorists to attack innocent people locally, regionally and universally?

We love America! We're Americans Muslims, and we've been here in America since the founding fathers of the United State of America established this nation till now.

I love you all!

*Dr. Badal Kariye*

We've reincarnation of idea and development if and when we're not forgetting to contribute and share knowledge among us, and as the word police investigation methods for data and DNA analysis are still advancing for better solutions to unsolved crimes around the world.

I and my children got amenities and everything in the United State of America, and we will live in and stay the rest of our lives as long as God let's live in peacefully. We really thank to the generous American people and our new government – the United States of America.

No nation is better than another nation so, let's respect each!

Let's help each other for good!

"And I wish that someone will one day return my stolen newborn boy."

Goodbye.

www.ingramcontent.com/pod-product-compliance
Ingram Content Group UK Ltd.
Pitfield, Milton Keynes, MK11 3LW, UK
UKHW041935190726
13854UKWH00004B/1599

9 781312 768505